The Magnetic Mindset

Unlocking the Secrets of Influence & Persuasion

Thomas Allan

KFT Publishing

© Copyright 2023 - All rights reserved by Thomas Allan

The content contained within this book may not be reproduced, duplicated or transmitted without direct written permission from the author or the publisher.

Under no circumstances will any blame or legal responsibility be held against the publisher, or author, for any damages, reparation, or monetary loss due to the information contained within this book, either directly or indirectly.

Legal Notice:

This book is copyright protected. It is only for personal use. You cannot amend, distribute, sell, use, quote or paraphrase any part, or the content within this book, without the consent of the author or publisher, except as permitted by U.S. copyright law.

Disclaimer Notice:

Please note the information contained within this document is for educational and entertainment purposes only. All effort has been executed to present accurate, up to date, reliable, complete information. No warranties of any kind are declared or implied. Readers acknowledge that the author is not engaged in the rendering of legal, financial, medical or professional advice. The content within this book has been derived from various sources. Please consult a licensed professional before attempting any techniques outlined in this book.

By reading this document, the reader agrees that under no circumstances is the author responsible for any losses, direct or indirect, that are incurred as a result of the use of the information contained within this document, including, but not limited to, errors, omissions, or inaccuracies.

ISBN: 978-0-6457786-2-5

Contents

Dedication	V
Introduction	1
Part 1: Magnetic Vision	4
1. The Human Need for Validation	5
2. The Psychology Behind Being Likable	12
3. Why Selling Is the Worst Way to Win Customers	19
4. How to Get Others to Buy Into Your Vision	24
Part 2: Magnetic Conversations	34
5. Tell Me a Little About Yourself	35
6. The Story of Who They Are	45
7. How to Find Like-Minded People	56
8. Build Your Personal Brand	65
Part 3: Magnetic Presentations	73
9. Techniques to Persuade Customers	74
10. What's Your Follow-Up?	83
11. What You Can Learn From Steve Jobs	90
12. A Crash Course on Public Speaking	98
Part 4: Magnetic Culture	108
13. Culture Starts With You	109
14. What Does a Positive Work Culture Look Like?	120
15. Get Out of Your Employees' Way	127

16. Go Big On Rewards	136
Conclusion	143
References	145
Also By	157
About Author	158

For all the people motivated to improve themselves, move from a fixed mindset, develop a growth mindset and perfect a magnetic mindset.

You make the world a better place to be.

Introduction

The real beginning of influence comes as others sense you are being influenced by them—when they feel understood by you—that you have listened deeply and sincerely, and that you are open. –Stephen R. Covey

Think about a best friend. Someone whom you would consider a "ride or die." What is it about that individual you appreciate? Is it their sense of humor, loyalty, or laid-back personality?

I'm sure you could create a long list of qualities that you appreciate about them, but I would like to suggest that none of those qualities would capture the essence of what keeps your relationship solid. The real reason why you would sacrifice a kidney for your best friend is that you know without a shadow of a doubt that your best friend would sacrifice a kidney for you.

Not the answer you wanted to hear, right? But here's something you may have forgotten about yourself as a human being—you are constantly looking out for your survival. You might not live in the jungle, but deep in the crevices of your brain, you still have an animal instinct. What draws you to people (and what draws people to you) is being liked or likable. This is a core survival need.

Imagine being in an environment where everyone gave you the cold shoulder, and building relationships felt like counting grains of sand. How open and comfortable would you be? Would it be possible to have meaningful conversations with others that gradually build trust? If you needed help, would you feel confident enough to ask for it? Your brain, being so overwhelmed with the cold reception, would activate survival mode. Your levels of stress and anxiety would rise, and the only thing on your mind would be finding the nearest exit!

As a leader, you may have taken for granted how important it is to be liked and likable. Perhaps when you were envisioning the executive suite on the top floor of the building, you saw yourself sitting in the 150 square feet office alone. While the position of CEO or senior manager is isolating, what you may not have considered are the relationships you would need to build in order to sustain your success.

Your vision cannot manifest or sustain itself. It requires cross-organizational teams to come together and bring it to life. Being liked and likable is how you form long-lasting connections and inspire the kind of devotion where an employee or customer would sacrifice a kidney for you or your business. Aren't those the kinds of connections you desire?

The Magnetic Mindset is the modern leader's guide to building and nurturing relationships with all relevant stakeholders. The value of this book is in how it focuses on changing how you think about human connection. To gain true influence and master the art of persuasion, you must look at relationships differently.

For example, if you have always seen employees as people who are paid to perform certain duties, you might start to see them as business partners or collaborators who creatively solve problems and translate your vision into products and services. This shift in mindset has the ability to change how you relate to and motivate your teams. It can also improve the way your teams respond to your leadership style.

While the focus of this book is leadership in business, the principles taught here can be applied to other aspects of your life, such as gaining influence with friends, family members, or other business and society leaders. The benefit of reconditioning your mind and seeing relationships differently is that you can adjust your approach in any kind of relationship, anytime and anywhere!

Having served as a leadership expert and business consultant for top organizations for over thirty tears, I have learned a vast amount of knowledge on human behavior. I have also seen examples of effective and ineffective leadership and the breakdown of trust that the latter can cause. When I am invited to facilitate team building or diversity training, I am always taken aback by the disconnect between employees and employers. What is clear to see is that neither party knows what the other needs and how to begin the process of building genuine relationships.

These experiences are what inspired me to write this book. Over the course of 14 chapters, I will draw on my extensive experience and expertise to help you develop the mindset and skills needed to become an effective leader. From understanding the principles of influence and persuasion to learning how to lead and inspire others, this book is packed with practical strategies and insights that can help you become a magnetic leader.

Whether you are an aspiring leader or an experienced manager looking to take your leadership skills to the next level, *The Magnetic Mindset* is the ultimate guide to unlocking your leadership potential!

Part 1: Magnetic Vision

Connect to the Needs and Desires of Others

Chapter One

The Human Need for Validation

We crave for the good opinion of the world, in which we don't believe and tremble in the face of its condemnation, which we despise and condemn in our hearts. –Hermann Sudermann

Do People Need Validation?

In 1943, psychologist Abraham Maslow presented what he called the "Hierarchy of Needs" in a research paper about human motivation. Five categories of needs were ranked on a pyramid in the following order (Sampath, 2021):

First tier: Physiological needs

Second tier: Safety needs

Third tier: Social needs

Fourth tier: Esteem needs

Fifth tier: Self-actualization

Maslow described the "esteem needs" (fourth tier) as developing from the ego. Only after the basic needs like shelter, income, and intimate relationships had been checked off could the individual start thinking about self-respect and self-esteem. According to him, esteem needs had two components: developing deeper trust in one's self and receiving validation from others.

Being validated by other human beings reinforces safety and social needs. This is because no man exists alone. You are born into a family, learn in the classroom, socialize in friendship circles, and work in teams. Receiving validation from other human beings provides a sense of belonging that makes you feel accepted and comfortable within the group or community.

The reason why some people rubbish the claim that we all need validation is because the thought of needing acceptance from others makes us feel vulnerable. When you approach a group of friends, for example, there is always a possibility that you may be rejected. Opening yourself up to that possibility is terrifying; you would rather develop a thick skin and approach people as though you didn't care what they thought about you. But even after going through those great lengths to hide your vulnerability, it wouldn't change your biological instinct to look for confirmation and support from your environment.

Seeking validation isn't a sign of weakness or desperation. It also shouldn't be confused with seeking approval. While these two experiences might look the same, the intentions are different. When you seek validation, you are looking for external confirmation that who you are and what you value is acceptable. You desire to feel that your thoughts and emotions matter in order to freely express yourself without shame. Healthy and reciprocal relationships tend to naturally offer validation and make you feel comfortable being yourself.

Seeking approval, on the other hand, is about looking to others to set the standards for who you are and what you believe. Instead of going out into the world with a strong sense of self, core values, and solid boundaries, you go out feeling empty and needing others to tell you what is acceptable or unacceptable. Their "Yes" gives you assurance, and their "No" feels like a heavy punch to the face. Ouch!

To prevent seeking the approval of others, you need to spend time getting to know yourself; who you are, what you believe, and what you desire out of life. You cannot depend on others to know this personal information about you because they simply don't live in your skin. Once you are clear about who you are, you can go out into the world and look for relationships that provide validation.

How to Make Employees Feel Seen

As a manager or leader of an organization, it is your responsibility to bring out the best in your team. The best way to do this is to constantly provide validation.

Now, you may be thinking, "Isn't this a two-way street?" The answer is no.

Leaders understand that with their positions comes a lot of authority—that in and of itself is enough validation. They don't need employees to confirm their thoughts and feelings because, as the "boss," they call the shots. This is why true leaders refuse to stand in the spotlight and would much rather provide opportunities for their employees to shine.

Validating employees isn't about inflating their egos but instead showing recognition of their work and performance. In other words, you make them feel seen and accepted as a valuable member of the team or organization. Several studies have shown that employees who receive constant validation report increased engagement at work. However, leaders are still unsure of how to make their employees feel seen.

The first place to start would be to assess whether you are providing enough support to bring out the best in your team. For instance, have you provided enough structure, rules and expectations, performance metrics, and rewards and recognition? Below are some questions to consider:

- Do employees know what is expected of them at work? What evidence can you show for it?

- Do employees know who their immediate supervisor is? Have they been told whom to reach out to for direct questions and concerns?

- Do employees know what targets they need to reach to earn rewards and recognition? Are these targets realistic and achievable? Have they been clearly articulated and encouraged?

- Do employees have the resources to complete their work every day? For instance, do they have enough time, support, budget, and skills/knowledge to produce high-quality results?

- Are employees encouraged to pursue personal and professional development? Does the culture at work promote the well-being and success of employees?

When leaders think about validating employees, they assume that monetary benefits are the best way to communicate how much they value their team. However, research by McKinsey shows that employees leave their jobs because of uncaring leaders, unsustainable work expectations, and little to no career development opportunities (Chodyniecka et al., 2022). What this means is that aside from a paycheck, employees desire to work in an organization that prioritizes their growth and well-being.

So, what are some of the non-monetary ways to validate employees? Below are five suggestions:

Pay Attention

Attentive listening is one of the best ways to validate another person. It entails dropping whatever you are working on, making eye contact, and listening to what the next person is communicating (verbally and nonverbally). It isn't always easy to pay attention, especially on busy days when you have a long list of tasks and not enough time to get through them all. However, just think about the cost of not paying attention and how many delays or misunderstandings could result when you aren't fully present in conversations or meetings. Plus, how would your employee walk away feeling after being ignored, shown the hand, brushed off, or told to cut their message short?

Practice Mirroring

Mirroring is a communication technique that ensures you understand what the next person is saying. The process involves repeating what you believe you heard back to the speaker, such as saying, "If I heard correctly, you said…" or "From what I gather, you feel…" This technique is especially useful when employees express their concerns or challenges and look to you for support and guidance. Note that you don't have to share the same thoughts and feelings as them to validate what they are saying and make them feel respected.

Notice Nonverbal Cues

According to the 7–38–55 rule, 7% of communication is in words, 38% is in the voice, and 55% is in body language (Michail, 2020). This means that about 93% of communication is nonverbal (without words). When validating your employees, be mindful of what they may be expressing to you through nonverbal cues, like facial expressions and gestures. Show them that you are paying attention by mentioning what you see.

For instance, if an employee stares at you in silence after you ask a question, that may signal confusion or uncertainty. In response, you might say, "I can see that I lost you there. Would you like me to repeat my question in a different way?" Or when an employee looks disengaged in a meeting, you can call them aside afterward and say, "I saw that you were not present in the meeting. Is everything okay?"

Show Empathy

Traditionally, empathy has never been considered one of the contributing factors to employee engagement and productivity. However, more organizations are waking up to the reality that their employees are human, and their mental and physical well-being impact the bottom-line. Due to increasing social and economic pressures, workers are also being more open about their need for empathetic leadership. According to a Businessolver's study, 92% of employees reported they would stay at their current job if their leader was empathetic, and 82% of employees would leave their current job if they found a more empathetic leader (Anderson, 2022).

You can show empathy by stepping inside your employees' shoes and imagining their experiences of coming to work, carrying out their duties, and making time for other aspects of their life. Imagine how they might be affected by the decisions you carry out or the stress they may be under due to personal issues. Create psychological safety at work by creating an open-door policy or establishing communication channels for various issues. Encourage your team to share their grievances and demonstrate a willingness to help them solve their problems.

Show Equality

There is typically a hierarchical structure in every organization. This structure should ideally be used to organize workers, not determine how they are treated. Regardless of where an employee ranks at work, it is important for them to feel valued. Not only will this positively impact their performance, but they will also feel comfortable sharing thoughts and ideas. The best way to show equality is to treat each employee the same, regardless of their position or your relationship with them.

Consider what kind of values you would like to model in front of your employees, and be intentional about displaying those values to the lowest and highest-ranking employees in the organization. For example, if one of your values is integrity, be quick to apologize when you have made a mistake and always deliver on your promises.

A good way to assess if you are treating employees equally is this: Ask employees to write down five keywords that describe you or your leadership style. There should be similarities in how employees describe you. If not, you have an opportunity to investigate where the discrepancies lie and improve your leadership approach.

In Summary

Validation is a fundamental human need that helps us feel confident in who we are and find our place within groups, workplaces, or communities. Your employees seek validation to feel accepted within the organization and competent in their abilities. There are a number of non-monetary ways to make your employees feel seen and respected, such as listening attentively, noticing nonverbal cues, and showing empathy. These may seem like small acts, but they can go a long way in deepening the relationship with your team.

Chapter Two

The Psychology Behind Being Likable

Harnessing likability is about uncovering what is authentically likable—in you, in the other person, in your connection. –Michelle Tillis Lederman

The People's President

Leaders are constantly worried about their reputations, particularly what their employees, partners, and clients think of them. This isn't due to the obsessive need for approval but rather their desire to gain influence.

To get to the top of any corporate ladder or industry, you need to be likable. Notice that I didn't mention graduating from Harvard or serving in the military—these are useful accomplishments to solidify your brand but aren't what make people like you.

Think for a moment about the employees you have recently hired or partners you have signed contracts to work with. Could you imagine yourself having coffee with these people or working alongside them in a small office cubicle? Your answer will certainly be "yes" because, as a human being, you subconsciously gravitate toward—and seek to help—people that you like.

The news of the first black President of the United States of America made waves across the country. Being born to a Kenyan father and American mother from Kansas, Obama's presidency was in many ways a symbol of a post-racial America. Yet not all Americans were ready for this change.

From as early as his 2008 presidential campaigns, many right-wing detractors expressed their disapproval of a man of color holding the highest office in the land. However, Obama never allowed attacks on his race to define his leadership. In a 2012 interview, he said, "I'm not the president of black America. I'm the president of the United States of America" (Dingle, 2012).

Over a series of events throughout his presidency, Obama was able to win the hearts of many Americans. When he left office in 2016, he had achieved a presidential approval rating of 57%, which was 23 percentage points higher than former President George W. Bush when he left office (Gallup, 2016). His secret for gaining the approval of ordinary Americans was to show vulnerability—something that was not typical of a man holding the most powerful position in society.

Below is just a snapshot of events where Obama was caught showing vulnerability:

- In 2012, Obama gave a speech in memory of the 6 teachers and 20 students that were murdered in Sandy Hook Elementary School. During his address, he shed tears while expressing how heartbroken the nation was. Four years later, he would shed tears again during a speech about gun violence.

- President Obama attended the funeral of Reverend Clementa Pinckney in 2015. While he was on stage reading the eulogy, he decided to sing Amazing Grace. The crowd cheered and rose from their seats to sing along with him. He ended his speech by saying, "May God continue to shed his grace on the United States of America."

- White House photographer, Pete Souza, captured a moment when a small boy named Jacob Philadelphia asked to touch Obama's hair. "I want to know if my hair is like yours," the little boy said. The President gave him permission to touch it and then asked him what he thought. "Yes, it does feel the same," the boy responded. This photo became a symbol of Obama's commitment to addressing race relations.

Obama understood that likability had nothing to do with having a perfect image. The way that he would positively influence ordinary Americans wasn't through a squeaky-clean image but rather by showing his humanity and embracing his strengths and weaknesses.

What Is the Pratfall Effect?

The Pratfall Effect is a theory that suggests highly competent people are more likable when they make everyday mistakes, like spilling coffee, saying something socially inappropriate, or being forgetful, than those who don't. The theory was discovered by social psychologist Elliot Aronson.

He hypothesized that people yielding a lot of power could become more likable by making a pratfall. A pratfall can be described as an embarrassing mistake, which can be seen as comical by others. His study consisted of 48 college-aged male participants who were divided into four groups.

Each group was told to listen to a tape recording of an individual answering trivia questions as an audition to participate in a TV game show. There were four types of people who were answering these trivia questions (Brescia University, 2017):

- A superior person.

- An average person.

- A superior person who made a pratfall.

- An average person who made a pratfall.

The participants were also told background information about the people answering questions. For instance, the superior person was academically gifted and a typical high-achiever who played in sports teams and held prestigious positions at school. In contrast, the average person earned average grades at school and unfortunately didn't make sports teams, nor did they hold prestigious positions at school.

After watching the videos, the participants were asked to answer questions on their impressions of the speakers. The findings revealed that superior individuals were seen as likable when they made a mistake. However, surprisingly, average individuals were seen unfavorably when they committed the same blunder.

What this experiment showed is that it is okay to be imperfect. In fact, showing human fallibility might earn you more respect, especially being someone in a position of authority.

Nevertheless, the mistakes you make cannot be superficial—purposefully committed to show perceived weaknesses. They must be as natural as misplacing your keys or spilling ketchup on a crisp white shirt. In essence, pratfalls work when you are simply being yourself around others instead of constantly self-monitoring.

Finding Common Ground

A few years ago, I was contacted by a startup tech company that had hit a wall. Their issue wasn't the lack of sales since the business was able to make a six-figure revenue on a monthly basis, but rather the lack of employee growth.

The CEO, who was an innovative and dedicated leader, did an outstanding job at picking some of the most talented workers in the tech industry. However, after assigning the workers into teams, he would often micro-manage them and demand things to be done his way.

What he didn't realize was that with each passing day, he was losing more and more influence over his employees. They were discouraged by the lack of trust and collaboration given by their boss. After a sit-down conversation with him, we both came to the conclusion that being "right" wasn't always the best way to lead employees. He needed to learn how to be relatable and teachable so that he could validate his talented employees and make them feel as though their contributions mattered.

Nobody will remember how many times you were right or wrong. However, they will certainly remember how you made them feel. Influential leaders know that by virtue of holding so much authority, they are looked at differently from others. Therefore, to be more likable, they deliberately humble themselves and seek to find common ground with their employees.

Finding common ground does not necessarily mean identifying shared values and interests. It is about listening attentively to the other person so you can find something to agree on. For example, instead of dismissing or scrutinizing an idea presented by one of your team members, you can look for aspects of the idea to agree on. Your opinion may remain different from theirs, but you are still able to see the situation from the other person's point of view.

The reason why finding common ground makes you likable is that you are able to forget about yourself for a few minutes and think in terms of mutual benefits. In other words, you are proactively looking for ways to validate and confirm what the other person is communicating, which makes them feel valued and respected. Finding common ground can also help to diffuse conflict and turn heated debates into healthy disagreements—all because the other person feels seen and heard, despite not sharing the same outlook.

There are a few communication tactics that can help you find common ground and validate others. These include:

Focus On the Big Picture

Whenever you are communicating with someone, keep the big picture in mind. Get a general sense of where they are coming from and the main point they are trying to convey. For example, if an employee expresses their concern about a new company policy and spends five minutes explaining why they believe the policy is wrong, the big picture to keep in mind is that they disapprove of the changes and seek to negotiate better terms and conditions.

What you can say: "I hear that you are not a fan of the new policy. Perhaps we can discuss potential improvements to the policy together?"

Sell the Why

When presenting ideas or making decisions on behalf of the company, there will be some employees, customers, or business partners who disagree. Please note that they are not disagreeing with you as an individual but rather "what" you are pitching or presenting. To persuade them and find common ground, you can shift their attention to the "why" behind your message. Selling the "why" is about communicating value and purpose. Since values and purpose are universal concepts, you are more likely to win people over and get them to buy into your ideas or decisions.

What you can say: "The reason why I am passionate about this upcoming change is because it promises to create more work opportunities within the organization."

Commit to Results, Not Specific Outcomes

Have you ever heard of the saying, "There is more than one way to skin a cat?" It can be interpreted to mean there is more than one way of doing something. When collaborating with others, remind yourself of this saying. Be mindful of the fact that your team members may offer suggestions that look different from yours but still achieve the same results. Don't be ashamed to go along with someone else's suggestion if it is better than yours. Instead of seeking to place your stamp on a proposal, focus on the results you hope to accomplish as a team.

What you can say: "I am so impressed with your idea because it can help us increase business sales while saving 30% costs."

Acknowledge Differences

Acknowledging differences is a sign of authenticity. It shows the other person that you are comfortable being yourself and standing up for what you believe. Nonetheless, differences in opinion don't mean you can't find common ground.

While not sharing the same thoughts or feelings, you can still express the desire to learn more about the other person's viewpoint.

What you can say: "Unfortunately, we will not be able to increase your salary by 5% this year. However, I am curious to find out from you how else we can reward you for your outstanding contributions to the company."

Acknowledge Positive Developments

Sometimes, you are unable to agree on a way forward, but through open dialogue, you are able to make significant progress. To encourage more honesty and negotiations to take place, acknowledge the positive developments that have occurred. Show the other person how far you have come to reach this stage of planning together. Present the positive developments as a win-win situation for both of you.

What you can say: "I know that we have gone back and forth on this decision, but I would like to show appreciation for how far we have come."

In Summary

You shouldn't feel guilty for wanting to be liked by your employees, customers, and partners. After all, the only way to grow your business is to get others to willingly follow your lead. However, increasing likability isn't as obvious as you might think. For instance, instead of a perfect leader, employees want to see your imperfections; and rather than always having the answers, they want you to lean back and acknowledge what they bring to the table.

Chapter Three

Why Selling Is the Worst Way to Win Customers

It's no longer about interrupting, pitching, and closing. It is about listening, diagnosing and prescribing. –Mark Roberge

The Right and Wrong Way to Sell a Pen

The whole point of being likable, from a sales perspective, is to convincingly pitch your products and services to potential customers. There is a famous scene in the film, *The Wolf of Wall Street* where Jordan Belfort (played by Leonardo DiCaprio), a successful stockbroker, challenges a group of amateur salesmen by asking them to sell him a pen.

He walks over to each one and hands them a pen, asking for their best sales pitch. They look at the pen and begin to give a list of characteristics:

- "The pen is shiny."

- "The pen is easy to write with."

- "This is a beautiful pen."

Looking unimpressed, he walks away. The group of salesmen are unable to provide the answer he is looking for. Only one person is able to convincingly sell the pen, and that is one of Belfort's trusted salesmen. Similarly to others, he is given the pen and asked to sell it.

The salesman looks at the pen and says, "Do me a favor; write your name on that napkin [pointing to a napkin in front of Belfort]." Belfort looks at the napkin and right back at the salesman. "I can't," he says, "I don't have a pen."

"Exactly," the salesman replies, "Supply and demand" (Wiener, 2021).

Top 5 Mistakes That Cause Your Sales Pitches to Be Rejected

Businesses need to make sales pitches to grab the attention of the right customers; however, customers hate anything that sounds remotely "pitchy."

Think about the last time you visited a shopping mall and were stopped by a group of promoters insisting that you sample their product or service. They may have been lovely people (of course, you were too agitated to notice that at the time), but that didn't take away from how lackluster and desperate their pitch sounded.

When you go in front of your audience and pitch a product or service, you are more likely to be met with resistance. However, this doesn't mean you should stop making pitches altogether. The problem with most businesses is that they move from "making initial contact with a potential customer" straight to "selling a product." The unexpected and often unwanted progression makes customers feel backed into a corner and suspicious about your claims.

Similar to any other relationship, the connection with your customers must start with a foundation of trust. Without this vital component, your messages won't carry influence. Once the trust has been established, you can go wild selling any product or service you believe your customer might like!

If you desire to build trust and create rejection-proof sales pitches, take a look at some of the common sales mistakes that cause customers to shut their ears and solutions that you can adopt in your business:

Mistake 1: Failing to Understand Your Customers' Needs

When you aren't clear about your customers' needs, you won't have a specific problem to help them solve by purchasing your products or services. Pitches that don't communicate an understanding of the customer, their lifestyle, habits, and core values tend to come across as shallow or uninspiring.

Remember that if your unique selling point is the product or service itself, then you are competing with hundreds of other similar businesses in your market, whose products or services may be smarter, cheaper, and more aesthetically pleasing than yours.

What to do: Demonstrate your ability to understand the issues your customer is faced with. Instead of making promises or talking about the benefits of your products or services, get straight into presenting the solutions and clearly laid out interventions that make sense and are convincing enough to get your customers to trust you.

Mistake 2: Talking "AT" Your Customer

The reason why traditional marketing tactics like direct mail or handouts can sometimes feel cold is because they promote a one-way conversation. They talk at the customer instead of talking to the customer. We tend to forget just how much access consumers have to information. Unlike pre-internet days, they can educate themselves on businesses within a matter of seconds.

Therefore, they don't need another lecture or lengthy document explaining what they already know. What they desire most is to feel a connection with your business, to know that you aren't just selling products but actually care about enhancing their quality of life.

What to do: Get rid of the generic business slides or brand messages that sound hollow and don't encourage engagement. Replace them with intentional presentations or messages that encourage dialogue and continued collaboration with customers. It is important for your customers to feel like you are a part of their lives and aren't about to go anywhere soon. Speak about the topics and interests they care about, ask questions, be playful, and find as many ways to nurture those relationships!

Mistake 3: Not Using Storytelling

I have seen many adverts online and offline where the purpose of the ad was missed. Whoever was in charge of the copy forgot an important aspect of sales—telling a story. Information alone won't convince customers to part with their hard-earned money unless, of course, you are selling a cure for a chronic illness! But generally, customers are driven by emotion when making purchasing decisions.

Telling stories is your way of relating to your potential customers on an emotional level. Not only does this make your business seem more humane, but it can also get them to act on impulse. Really captivating stories told with sincerity can even convert first-time customers into brand ambassadors since they see themselves reflected in your business' values and messages.

<u>What to do:</u> When drafting your pitch, take some time to think about what story you can tell that can resonate with your audience. It could be a real story about your business (i.e., sharing memorable moments with employees and customers) or a story about relatable life events that customers can relate to.

Let this story be the base of your pitch—the reason people stop scrolling and take a few seconds to engage with your social media post or drop whatever they are doing and listen to your presentation.

Mistake 4: Making False Claims

Even though customers tend to make emotional purchasing decisions, they are not naive. With hundreds of businesses marketing similar products or services, many customers are looking for the most reliable ones to partner with. Reliability means delivering goods that match what you advertised and fulfilling every promise you made.

<u>What to do:</u> Under-delivering on your promises can jeopardize the trusting relationship you are seeking to build with customers. Even if your products or services aren't as sophisticated as your competitors, set realistic expectations. Take realistic photos, post honest reviews and testimonials, and budget extra time and costs to deliver the goods to your customers.

Mistake 5: Being Too Pushy

According to the "Rule of 7," customers need to see or hear your marketing messages seven times before they are driven to take action. Realistically, this could mean waiting several weeks or months before converting a prospective customer into a paying one. Being aggressive with your pitch, like sending multiple emails per week, can make you come across as being pushy and inauthentic. While it is good to keep the conversation going with each prospective customer, it is also necessary to be patient.

What to do: Know when to turn pitch mode on and off. It is not necessary to sell something every time you make contact with your customers. Another rule that can help you plan content is the rule of thirds. This rule states that one-third of your content should be personal and allow customers to get to know your business, another third should point to relevant third-party content (i.e., articles and videos), and another third should promote your products or services.

In Summary

There's no way of getting around it—you will need to make pitches to prospective customers. But since most customers hate being pitched to, it is important to learn how to sell yourself without actually selling yourself. Practicing validating your customers by understanding their needs and being likable by finding common ground (referring to chapters 1 and 2) will help you get messages across in the most authentic and persuasive way.

Chapter Four

How to Get Others to Buy Into Your Vision

If you hire people just because they can do a job, they'll work for your money. But if you hire people who believe what you believe, they'll work for you with blood and sweat and tears. –Simon Sinek

Do You Have a Vision?

The word *vision* is derived from the Latin word "videre," which means *to see*. Managers and leaders who have a vision are able to see the long-term trajectory of the business, and what needs to be done today to arrive at a positive and profitable future.

Without a vision, it is difficult to measure the effectiveness of objectives or determine whether employees are doing enough to sustain and grow the business. Thus, in many ways, a vision becomes a standard that the entire organization upholds and seeks to promote.

There is an old story about Former President John F. Kennedy taking a tour of the NASA buildings in 1963. He walked through a particular hallway and came across a janitor mopping the floor. The President approached the janitor and asked what his role was at NASA. "Mr. President," the janitor replied, "I am sending a man to the moon!"

Was he really sending a man to the moon? Certainly not. That job would be assigned to the engineers. However, his response showed that he understood the vision of NASA, and had bought into it. As a result, he was able to perform his daily cleaning duties with a lot more rigor because there was a bigger purpose behind what he was doing.

An organization's vision is one of the first elements of its culture. There are so many aspects of the business that the vision informs, such as the attitude employees have toward their work, how different stakeholders relate to each other, and acceptable norms, habits, and behaviors in the workplace.

For example, IKEA's vision is "to create a better everyday life for the many people" (Peek, 2022). By "many people," the company not only considers their customers but also their employees. For instance, employees working at IKEA have reported receiving benefits like subsidized meals, Christmas gifts from Santa, interest-free loans, and even life insurance. The company also offers annual bonuses and opportunities for career advancement (Baxter-Wright, 2017).

There is no better tool to unite teams and the organization at large than creating and communicating a vision. This chapter will teach you how to create an impactful vision and get others to buy into it.

There Is No Vision Without Values

Values can be defined as moral standards that you live by. They inform what you deem acceptable or unacceptable behavior, what you consider to be a successful or an unsuccessful life, as well as what you aspire to achieve. Without core values, your life can feel uncertain, and you can get caught up in routines that are unproductive or unfulfilling.

According to author and entrepreneur Stan Slap, "the purpose of leadership is to change the world around you in the name of your values, so you can live those values more fully" (Good Reads, n.d.). What he means by this is that your personal values are connected to your vision—this could be the vision for your personal or professional life.

What you hope to achieve has everything to do with what you believe is possible and what you believe you are capable of. Therefore, before crafting a vision, it is important to take a moment and consolidate your values. If you value excellence, for example, you may envision yourself becoming a high achiever or leading a top-performing company. Now, of course, this is an extraordinary vision that will take mastering certain skills, however, since you are anchored by something that deeply matters to you (i.e., the purpose of excellence), you are able to push forward and do what is necessary to achieve it.

The same applies when creating business values and setting a business vision. The values that you establish for your business will determine the kind of future you envision for it. If you believe in diversity, you are more likely to create policies and a work culture that embraces people from all racial, social, and cultural backgrounds. Of course, you would need to be intentional about living out this value, but the fact remains that it is a standard that you deeply care about.

Your business vision is the "what" you are chasing, but your business values are the "why." Having a strong enough "why" will ensure that your organization is able to withstand obstacles that it is confronted with because of being built upon solid principles.

Crafting Your Value Statement

You may be sold on the idea of having business values but aren't sure where to start. There are four main functions business values need to serve in order for them to be effective:

- Your values need to help employees learn what is acceptable and unacceptable behavior in the workplace, and the general approach they are required to have toward their work.

- Your values must eloquently express what your company stands for and what it means to be an employee at the organization (i.e., your values need to give employees a professional identity).

- Your values must inform the work culture enforced in your company, as well as the practices that can help employees learn how to relate to one another.

- Your values must be fair, inclusive, and stable even when management changes.

When you look at a value list of an organization, you may see words like transparency, diversity, accountability, openness, and continuous learning. These words represent what that particular organization prizes as its most important principles to live and work by. Depending on your company's direction, you will also have a value list that is carefully curated to reflect the principles behind your vision.

The following exercise will assist you in crafting your unique value statement:

1. Write down keywords to describe your company.

2. Remove those keywords that competitors can also claim. Rewrite your list to include what makes your company unique.

3. How would you like external stakeholders to perceive your company? What thoughts or feelings do you want them to associate with your business?

4. What does "great work" look like for your company? What would you need to achieve? How would employees need to perform as individuals and in teams?

5. What important qualities should employees display at work?

6. What do you believe are the most important determinants of high performance? What high-performing qualities do you desire employees to adopt?

7. As a leader, what do you believe are the most important qualities to display at work to get the most out of your employees? What attitudes

and behaviors would you need to adopt?

The answers to these seven questions will reveal recurring values that you treasure and believe define your company. Go over your responses and identify 3–10 values. Write them down.

From the list above, find 3–5 common themes that you can group your values under. For example, honesty, trust, and transparency could be grouped under "integrity."

Once you have the 3–5 themes, it is time to draft your value statement. A values statement could be a sentence or a descriptive paragraph that explains your fundamental principles and priorities as a business. A good value statement will be specific on how each value is linked to employer and employee behavior. For example, if one of your values is "collaboration" you would explain it in the following way: "We will work together to achieve shared goals." The more clear you are in describing each value, the easier it will be for the entire organization to follow.

Write down your value statement.

3 Steps to Create Your Vision

Now that you have formulated your value statement, you have a better sense of where you would like to see your business in the next 5–10 years. You are now ready to create a vision that will unite your organization and become the "North Star" that represents what you hope to achieve in the future.

Similar to the values exercise, you will need to create a separate vision statement. Your statement will be a culmination of your company mission, core values, and long-term goals. To simplify the process of creating your vision statement, you can follow these three steps:

Step 1: Determine Who to Consult

Establishing a vision for your organization is an extremely important decision that affects every aspect of your business. It is perfectly normal to brainstorm your vision with trusted business partners, mentors, or teams within your company. Some leaders, for example, hire consultancy firms to help them create compelling visions, and others prefer to collaborate with employees on constructing a shared vision that they will buy into. Even if you decide to create the vision alone, it won't hurt to get feedback and insights from employees before enforcing it.

Step 2: Define Your Future

Envision your company in 5–10 years' time. Think about the milestones you would have reached by then, how big your company would have grown, how many new products or services you would offer, and your reputation in the industry. Next, answer the following questions to describe your vision:

1. You wake up five years later and walk into your office. Describe what you see. Mention the size of your company, the culture of your workplace, various teams or departments that exist, etc.

2. After greeting your employees, you step into your office and see a hot cup of coffee and today's newspaper sitting on your desk. Your company has made the front page. Describe the headline and news story that you are being recognized for.

3. Your eyes wander across the room and gravitate toward a few plaques and awards on a side table. Describe what your company has been honored and awarded for, and how you were able to achieve that milestone as an organization.

4. You look at your watch and realize you have a staff meeting in the next 5 minutes. Fortunately, the meeting room is just next door. As you enter the room, you see X amount of employees waiting for you. Describe your relationship with the team, how they relate with each other, as well as your collective approach to solving problems and working on company goals.

Step 3: Write Your Vision Statement

At this point, you have plenty of information to use to create an inspiring vision statement. Remember, your vision statement will be a culmination of your company mission, core values, and long-term goals. Based on the vision statement you crafted and the short visualization exercise you completed above, write down a descriptive vision statement of the future you intend to make a reality.

Note that your vision statement can be a simple sentence or several sentences long. Instead of focusing on the length, try to make the vision as clear, specific, and motivating as possible.

Here is an example of a short vision statement by Tesla (Brex, n.d.):

"To accelerate the world's transition to sustainable energy"

And here is an example of a mid-length vision statement by Coca-Cola (Coca-Cola Company, 2023):

"Our vision is to craft the brands and choice of drinks that people love, to refresh them in body & spirit. And done in ways that create a more sustainable business and better-shared future that makes a difference in people's lives, communities, and our planet."

Write down your company's vision statement.

How to Communicate Your Vision

Until a vision is shared with others, it exists as a few words written on a page. What gives your vision power is instilling the same passion and drive in others, so they can start moving toward the attainment of your future goals.

Communicating your vision is also about getting employees to commit to working and relating to each other in a certain way. They need to know what matters to the organization and feel the same strong desire within themselves.

While you are not a master magician*, who can twirl a wand and make others believe in your vision, you can apply certain strategies to communicate and get others to buy into the vision. These strategies include:

1. Telling a story

How do you capture people's attention? By telling a great story. Help your employees understand what inspired the vision, what makes you confident that you can achieve it, and how they can get involved. Focus on describing the emotional connection you have to the vision, and make your story relatable.

For example, every employee can relate to having a dream as a child to one-day building something phenomenal or failing several times before getting up and doing things differently. They are more likely to remember the impactful story than a slideshow with the vision statement pasted.

2. Create an elevator pitch

You won't always have time to share your story with everyone you meet. For instance, when networking with other business people, it may not be appropriate to share your story. This is when your elevator pitch comes into play. The pitch is a short (less than a minute) summary of your business' vision. It is meant to be brief and provide just enough information to differentiate you from competitors.

A good trick is to practice your elevator pitch regularly so that whenever you are asked about your company, you can immediately start talking. Test out a few elevator pitches with friends, family, or colleagues, and choose the one that effectively sells your business without selling it (refer to chapter 3).

3. Share the vision through multiple channels

Talking about your vision is one way of communicating it, but this strategy alone won't be sufficient to get stakeholders to buy in. Identify the various spaces where people can interact with your business, such as your physical office, website, emails, social media pages, and product packaging. Find ways to place your vision in those spaces using different methods.

For example, in the office, you might have signage with your vision against a wall or include the vision on your corporate presentation slides. On your website, the vision can appear on the homepage or "About Us" page and on emails as part of your email signature or incorporated in your newsletters. Play around with different placements, but ensure that it looks professional.

4. Ask for feedback

Get feedback from your employees about the vision. Focus on listening to how much they understand the vision rather than their likes or dislikes of the vision. An employee is more likely to resist following your vision if they misunderstand your intentions or are unclear about how they might be affected. Feedback shows you where the gaps lie and what you will need to do to improve how you communicate the vision with employees.

5. Back up your vision with your behaviors

Your vision may be powerful, but at the end of the day, employees will be positively influenced by your behaviors. When you act inconsistently with the vision, they may doubt how much achieving those aims matters to you and whether the values you advocate are genuine. To get others to buy into your vision, you need to model consistent behavior and show them that it is possible to achieve it.

Repeating these communication strategies will create familiarity and silence the doubts of those who may be resistant to change. Successful repetition requires using different tactics to ingrain the vision in your employees' memory. Play around with different forms, channels, and elements (i.e., text, visual, audio, etc.) to help your vision gain traction and become a source of inspiration in your organization.

In Summary

In order for internal and external stakeholders to willingly agree to pursue your vision, they must be persuaded. The best way to persuade them is to first get clear on your life and career principles. Your mindset and actions as a leader will inform how big you can dream and how much passion you can ignite in the hearts of others. Thereafter, creating a vision is a matter of identifying your core business values, defining the future of your company, and using different communication strategies to get others' buy-in.

Part 2: Magnetic Conversations

Share the Story of Who You Are

Chapter Five

Tell Me a Little About Yourself

Never forget what you are, for surely the world will not. Make it your strength. Then it can never be your weakness. Armour yourself in it, and it will never be used to hurt you. –George R.R. Martin

Everybody has a life story. Behind the charming smile, social awkwardness, or obsessive compulsive behavior, there is a story about who someone is, where they have been, and where they are heading in life. However, even though everybody has a life story, many are either blissfully unaware of theirs or feel uncomfortable embracing it.

For example, in the work environment, you might hide your story behind the professional self-image that you believe might get you ahead in your career. By only showing those aspects of yourself that are acceptable, you think that you will be able to build strong relationships with colleagues. But the truth is the professional self-image can work against you, especially when it is so disconnected from who you truly are.

You will remember in chapter 2, we spoke about the importance of being likable and some of the ways to go about achieving that. One of the points mentioned was showing authenticity by embracing strengths and weaknesses. We discovered that displaying an image of perfection worked against leaders because that made them less relatable. What employees really wanted to see was the leader's genuine personality.

It takes a lot of courage and self-awareness to be able to reveal who you truly are with others. The hardest part isn't so much about expressing yourself but first coming to terms with who you are and understanding your life story. Your life story is what gives meaning to your goals, achievements, and relationships. When you are unfamiliar or uncomfortable with it, you may struggle to organize your past experiences, build a strong sense of self, and envision a brighter future.

Your life story doesn't just help you express your personality—it shapes your personality. Depending on how you have made sense of your past, you will perceive reality in a particular way, and this will inform how you interact with others. It is, therefore, vital to understand how a life story is constructed and the impact it has on who you are and how you present yourself.

Below are a few facts about life stories that are borrowed from narrative psychology (Gregoire, 2013):

1. **Your life story evolves over time**
   You are not the same person you were 10–15 years ago because your life has changed significantly since then. With this same logic, it is important to realize that your life story has evolved with you and doesn't represent a version of you that no longer exists.
   Think of your life story as a movie with several different scenes. Each scene unfolds in a different setting, with different themes, actions, and characters. The final scene of the movie usually looks very different from how the movie began.

2. **Your current emotions inform how you tell the story**
   How you perceive your life story (whether you are satisfied or unsatisfied with who you are and where you currently are) is influenced by your emotional state. Whenever you are going through depressive periods in your life, you are more likely to have a negative perception of your story, whereas, during happier times, you may tend to reflect on your story with

more hope and optimism.

3. **Life stories are structured in sequence**
   In general, most people understand their life through a sequence: beginning, middle, and end. This is done to help the brain organize memories into periods, seasons, and chapters of your life. For example, you might refer to the "beginning" of your life when speaking about your childhood and the "middle" of your life when speaking about where you are today. Using this simple sequence will help you fill the missing gaps of your story and reflect on specific periods in your life.

4. **Redemption is a common theme in successful people's stories**
   Have you ever heard a wealthy man talk about their "rags to riches" story? Or describe how they went from experiencing a series of failures to achieving a breakthrough? The common theme in these stories is the concept of redemption, which is the act of being saved from evil, misfortune, or mistakes.
   The general sequence of a redemptive story is that things start off really badly and then, with time, skill, and exposure, become progressively better. Moreover, failure is often perceived as a catalyst for change, not the end of the road or a sign of personal weakness.

5. **You have control over your story**
   There are two types of people: Those who believe that life happens *to* them and those who believe that life happens *for* them. Out of the two, who do you think has more control over their life story?
   The fact is that at any point in your life, you can choose to modify your life story. You don't need more money, time, or skills to update your perception of your life. All you need is the desire to see things differently. When you notice that your current life story is inhibiting you in some way, such as preventing you from making genuine connections or expressing who you truly are, you can choose to tell a different story that feels more empowering.

How to Identify a Negative Life Story

A few years ago, I attended a leadership conference in Florida. In between the presentations, I got the opportunity to network with some of the attendees, who were mid-level and senior-level managers. We had casual conversations about the organization they worked for and how they were finding their roles.

One particular senior-level manager left an impression on me. His name was Derick, and he had been working in the finance industry for over 15 years. Being raised by a single mother in the projects of Houston, Texas, it was always his plan to escape poverty and succeed in the corporate world.

I found Derick's story inspiring and proceeded to ask him, "So, what's next?" He looked at me as though I had missed the point. For him, reaching senior-level management was the pinnacle of his success. He hadn't imagined going any farther than that. In fact, the thought of accomplishing anything more than what he already had triggered his insecurities.

Although he was able to escape poverty, he couldn't get away from the poverty mentality. You see, a poverty mentality has nothing to do with materialistic possessions. It has more to do with the tendency to reaffirm your lack. For instance, you might be afraid of networking because you think that you aren't smart enough to engage with other esteemed professionals. Or, despite your corporate success, you might be convinced that there are certain career goals that are "too big" for you.

This poverty mentality can also inform your outlook on life. Derrick, for example, placed unnecessary restrictions on his development because, deep down, he didn't believe he deserved an abundance of success (whatever that may have looked like for him). He also had the habit of speaking about his past as though he was still living it. Having such a limiting life story is what reinforced his poverty mentality and made it difficult to envision success beyond his current role.

The danger of not addressing a negative life story is that you will start to see the world (and yourself) from a distorted mirror. Not only will that place limits on who you are and how you relate to others right now, but it will also paint a miserable picture of the future.

We assume that every leader must have a positive life story, or else how could they have landed a leadership position? However, life stories are complex, and it is possible to have a high regard for yourself in one area of your life (e.g., competence) but a low regard for yourself in another area of your life (e.g., confidence). This is why it is common to find leaders who are so developed in one area but need significant work in another.

It is important for you to learn how to identify a negative life story. When you do this, you will be able to detect mindsets or beliefs that are weighing you down and reaffirm your fears or doubts. Once you find this negative life story, you will have the power to modify it and remove whatever mental or emotional barrier it was causing.

To make an illustration, let us go back to my friend Derick's story. His negative life story was rooted in his past. For some reason or another, Derrick was unable to separate himself from the story of poverty and lack. His life story reinforced the same kinds of struggles and constraints he experienced many years ago as a growing kid. In other words, psychologically, he was still holding onto his difficult past.

By identifying the negative life story, Derick would be able to dig deeper and look for harmful mindsets or beliefs that were keeping this story alive. One of them is a poverty mentality (as explained above); however, there may also be a sense of personal inadequacy that is holding him back. All of this information is useful because it can help Derick rewrite his story.

The same opportunity is now presented to you. Take a moment to think about a negative life story you may be telling yourself. It could be a story about your life, career, position at work, or capabilities. For example:

- "My life is tougher than everybody else's."

- "I'm not ready to pursue my goals."

- "I don't have enough time to pursue my goals."
- "I'm not a likable person."
- "I'm too old/young to work on that goal."
- "You can't trust anyone."
- "I'm never chosen/invited/considered by others."

Select only one story and answer the following questions:

1. What negative story have you been telling yourself? Which area of your life has it affected?
2. Where does this story come from? What past life events have informed it?
3. What has been the benefit of holding onto this story? What "comfort" has telling yourself this story brought you?
4. Dig deeper and identify harmful mindsets, attitudes, or beliefs that have reinforced this story. List as many as you can think of.
5. Envision the future if you continue to hold onto this story. Describe how your work, health, or relationships will look like.
6. Now, envision the future if you rewrite this story. Describe how your work, health, or relationships will look like.

6 Steps to Rewrite Your Life Story and Change Your Life

It may seem dramatic to think that by rewriting your life story you could change your life, but it isn't. The truth is the only thing that has kept you back from launching into your greatness is the story you keep telling yourself.

It isn't the lack of career growth, slow business sales, or networking opportunities that have gone bust. Your own story about your life has been the greatest influence on how you think, speak, behave, and make sense of the world and others.

Below are six steps that you can practice regularly to confront negative life stories and adjust how you perceive your life:

Step 1: Set Yourself as the Protagonist

A protagonist is the main character in a novel or production. They are usually who "life happens for" as opposed to "life happening to." The audience gets to understand the story from the protagonist's point of view rather than seeing it from the antagonist's—the one who is in conflict with or competes against the protagonist.

If you are not careful, you can tell your life story from the perspective of a victim or through the eyes of the person that caused you a lot of pain. Not only is this unfair to you, but it can also prohibit you from taking control of your life. You should be central in the plot of your life instead of taking on a lesser role.

Exercise: Think about a life story where you have cast yourself as the victim, bystander, observer, or any other lesser role. Rewrite the story and tell it through your own eyes, as the protagonist.

Step 2: Decide On a New Theme

Themes are important aspects of stories because they help to organize a writer's thoughts and ideas. All of the actions that unfold within a chapter or chapters are related to themes. If we had to break down the story of your life, we would be able to identify several themes that have occurred. These may include the theme of tragedy, failure, hope, and victory.

Each theme is important to almost "summarize" the various events you were experiencing at the time. Nonetheless, as your life situation changes, so does the theme; which is why you must constantly update your story's theme.

Exercise: Reflect on the current narrative of your life and identify a theme that might best represent your experience. Remember, you don't have to settle on a negative theme. If you like, you can choose to interpret your life circumstances from a positive perspective.

Step 3: End Chapters You Don't Need

Every story plot line has a beginning, middle, and end. How a chapter ends is just as significant as how it begins. When you close a chapter of your life, you are essentially tying loose ends and giving yourself closure for a period you have been through and overcome. It is also the time when you reflect on what you have learned from those past experiences and mentally prepare yourself to move on.

It is never easy to close chapters when you still have unresolved emotions about what happened and how it may have impacted you. Thus, before you can close the chapter, you must acknowledge the necessity of letting go.

Exercise: Recall an old chapter of your life that is still open. Write a compassionate letter to the younger version of yourself, explaining the importance of tying loose ends and moving forward. Provide benefits for seeking closure and accepting what has happened.

Step 4: Learn From the Villain

Every great hero story needs a villain because, without the opposition, the hero wouldn't be able to self-actualize. Perhaps it is ironic that some of the worst times of your life can lead to the greatest amount of personal growth. Adversity has a way of forcing you to open your eyes to the reality of life and change the way you think and relate to others.

If you have ever encountered a villain in your life, who may have been a friend, family member, or colleague, you ought to thank them for the indirect ways they forced you to grow. Instead of assuming that the only purpose they had to play in your story was to cause pain, consider that they may have been cast into your life story to teach you priceless life lessons.

Exercise: Think about a villain from your past who caused you a lot of pain. Mention at least five things they indirectly taught you about life.

Step 5: Change the Setting

A research study by the American Psychological Association (APA) found that people who work abroad become comparatively more creative than those who remain in the comfort of their towns and cities. This shows how changing locations can positively impact your life.

Fortunately, you don't need to physically relocate to improve your life story. All you need to do is mentally adjust the setting of your life. You wouldn't believe how common it is for leaders to still mentally identify as managers or for successful entrepreneurs to still see themselves as the struggling hustler who is trying to make ends meet. This is proof that your external environment can change while your internal environment (i.e., thoughts, beliefs, and emotions) remain stuck in the past.

To change the setting of your life, focus on embracing where you are. Mindfulness meditation can assist you with this shifting process! You can even recite positive affirmations to remind yourself of who you are and the upgraded life you are living (more on this later in the book).

Exercise: Describe your current life's setting, focusing on who you are, where you are, and what you have right now. The emphasis should be on recognizing what is here, instead of what you lost or what you desire. Pretend as though you are describing your current life to someone who doesn't know you; mention details about your personality, career, family, hobbies, etc.

Step 6: Improve Your Supporting Cast

The role of the supporting cast is essentially that—to support the protagonist in telling their story. While they play a lesser role in the story, the story wouldn't develop without them. Therefore, every main character needs a supporting cast to become the best version of themselves.

Reflect on the people who have been a part of the supporting cast in your life. How have these people impacted your story? Do you believe that your supporting cast is positively or negatively influencing the development of your story?

Just as much as you can rewrite your life story, you can also improve your supporting cast. This might include setting boundaries with difficult people, broadening your professional network and connecting with like-minded people, or investing in therapy to receive emotional support.

Exercise: Write down ways in which you can improve your supporting cast. For example, mention qualities that you will start to prioritize when looking for friends or business partners or professionals like doctors or mentors whom you can reach out to for support and guidance.

In Summary

When someone says, "Tell me about yourself," what they are asking is for you to share a summary of your life story. Life stories are how people connect and express their personalities. Traditionally, it was seen as taboo to share who you truly are at work, but nowadays, more leaders are finding that being open and forthcoming about who they are can make them more relatable.

Since your life story is not fixed, it is important to update it regularly. Each season of your life has its own theme, setting, villains, and supporting cast. Constantly remind yourself of who you are and where you are today so that your perceptions match your current reality.

Chapter Six

The Story of Who They Are

When we establish human connections within the context of shared experience, we create community wherever we go. –Gina Greenlee

See the World Through Somebody Else's Eyes

There is a story told by English author and screenwriter Douglas Adams about a specific incident in 1976 when he arrived early to catch a train (Bringle, 2013). Noticing that he had a lot of time on his hands, he bought a newspaper, hot coffee, and a packet of cookies to keep himself occupied.

Sitting across from him at the table was another gentleman who seemed to be waiting for a train too. Adams didn't think much about the gentleman except when he reached out for his packet of cookies, opened them, and grabbed one to eat. As it is the tradition of the English to be polite, Adams pretended not to see what was happening. Perhaps the gentleman had been waiting for several hours and became hungry. Who would deny a hungry person food?

To hint at his disapproval, Adams slid the packet toward himself and grabbed a cookie. About 15 minutes later, the gentleman stood up, helped himself to another cookie, and went back to his seat. The scene became awkward. How could Adam raise the issue about the cookies after the gentleman insisted on taking a second helping?

The two of them went back and forth, grabbing cookies after each other until crumbs remained inside the packet. The gentleman looked very uncomfortable, so he stood up and walked away. Moments later, Adams' train was announced, and he took the final sip of cold coffee and folded the newspaper. Nothing could have prepared him for what he found underneath his newspaper: A fresh and sealed packet of cookies that he had bought.

You can rest assured that when you are engaging with someone, they are interpreting your words and actions from their own worldview. Imagine that your words and actions are processed in their brain through a filter. This filter is constructed by their ideas, beliefs, mindsets, memories, and emotions. In essence, they don't hear or see what you are doing from your perspective but through their own.

A person's perspective informs their reality. When you are in a meeting or addressing a group of people, recognize that what you are saying is being understood differently. Why is this important to know as a leader? Because the success of your leadership is in the ability to share messages and influence others.

If the people you are leading are interpreting your messages through their mental filters, then you need to familiarize yourself with their worldview. Getting to know more about them and how they think and feel will allow you to modify your messages for greater impact.

There are three skills you can practice to help you see the world from someone else's perspective:

1. **Perspective-taking**

The first skill is known as perspective-taking. This involves looking at the situation from a different angle. In a boss-employee discussion, for example, you would metaphorically step out of your role as boss and see the situation from the employee's point of view. To practice taking on different perspectives, think of different people, and ask yourself:

- What do they care about?
- What do they fear?
- What gets them out of bed in the morning?

Notice how differently the world looks from another person's perspective, as well as how far off their perspective is from yours. Realize that for the majority of the time, these people are relating to you from that place or mentality.

2. Perspective-seeking

Perspective-seeking looks a little bit different from perspective-taking. Instead of imagining what someone else's reality looks like, you can go a step further and ask questions to understand their outlook better. What's great about this approach is that it can eliminate any assumptions you may have made about the person or their experience. Furthermore, you get an opportunity to clarify what you have heard, such as saying:

- If I hear you correctly, you are saying…
- When you say… Do you mean… ?
- Do you mind elaborating on that point?

The value of perspective-seeking is in understanding people who express different opinions than you. Being able to show curiosity in place of resistance can help to broaden your understanding of reality and appreciate where someone else is coming from. Note that perspective-seeking doesn't need to lead to agreement; however, at the very least, you are able to validate another person's experience.

3. Perspective-coordinating

The purpose of understanding different perspectives is to gather information about how others are experiencing the world. You can use this information to make informed decisions or improve the way you communicate ideas and thoughts to others. In other words, by understanding the filter from which an employee experiences the workplace, you can modify your messages and speak in a "language" they understand. This won't necessarily change your personal outlook, but it will help you explain your outlook in a more sympathetic and engaging way.

How to Become a Better Empathetic Listener

Research has shown that employees who believe they are free to express themselves are 4.6 times more likely to be engaged at work (Beheshti, 2019). To create this kind of culture or environment at work, it is important for leaders to learn how to validate employees by showing empathy.

The topic of empathy is usually a contentious one in the workplace because leaders and employees have a different understanding of what it entails. If you ask a leader to give you an example of how their organization shows empathy, they might tell you about the remuneration policy they have recently implemented. While this is a great initiative that shows consideration for workers, it isn't exactly what employees think of when it comes to empathy.

Ask any employee what empathy looks like in the workplace, and they will mention examples like being able to share personal issues with their manager and getting helpful advice, having flexible work schedules to create a better work-life balance, and being able to voice their concerns without fear of being judged or punished. If we could summarize how employees perceive empathy at work, it would be feeling accepted and supported regardless of their differences.

Empathetic listening is the gateway to empathy. It refers to the act of listening attentively to what another person is saying to get clues about how they are experiencing reality and the emotional impact that has on them. It is worth noting that this type of thinking is not the norm in the workplace or any kind of relationship. In his book *The 7 Habits of Highly Effective People*, Stephen R. Covey outlines the five levels of listening that people follow, which are:

1. Ignoring what the other person is saying.

2. Pretending to listen to the other person.

3. Selectively choosing which parts of the message you listen to.

4. Focusing on what the other person is saying.

5. Empathetically listening to what the other person is saying.

As you will notice, empathetic listening is the final stage that not many people reach. This isn't always due to dismissive or passive-aggressive behavior. Sometimes, it could be due to the many distractions that steal your attention, such as phone or email notifications, being preoccupied with thoughts, or attempting to multitask. Empathetic listening requires you to stop whatever you are doing, give your attention to another person, and connect to their experience.

Some leaders may find empathetic listening challenging because it demands more than listening attentively to what an employee is saying. They are encouraged to immerse themselves into the employees' reality and mirror their feelings back to them. For example, when an employee expresses their frustration about a work process, the leader is challenged to abandon their own need to be right or defend their decision and explore what the employee must be going through on a day-to-day basis. By letting go of their story and looking at the situation from the employee's perspective, they may be able to find common ground.

Another difficult aspect of empathetic listening is being aware of the other person's unconscious thoughts and feelings. Once again, this can be challenging for leaders because it requires them to suspend judgment and show sensitivity to what the employee may be going through. For example, on the surface, you may see an employee who is disengaged at work. However, if you step into their world and imagine the various stressors they may be experiencing, both at work and at home, you may start to interpret their silence or lack of initiative differently.

Improving your empathetic skills begins with an awareness that there is only one of you and one of each human being. No individual thinks or feels the same as the next person. While there may be similarities between people and teams, each individual must be seen as being unique. With this acknowledgment, it will be easier to practice the following three steps:

Create a Safe Space for Sharing

Emotional safety at work refers to the ability for employees to feel comfortable sharing their thoughts and feelings without fear of being judged. In such workplaces, ideas, concerns, and feedback is welcome. There is often a culture of collaboration in the form of brainstorming sessions, problem-solving as teams, and open forums where employees can leave suggestions or raise issues.

The first step to becoming an empathic leader is to create an emotionally safe workplace. You can do this by making openness or honesty one of your organizational values or part of your work culture. The permission to "think out loud" or openly challenge the status quo at work must come from the top in order for employees to feel safe speaking freely.

Think about some of the practices you can adopt to create emotional safety at work. Write your suggestions down below:

Acknowledge the Speaker's Feelings

What sets empathetic listening apart from active listening is the element of making observations of the other person's behavior and interpreting what you see. For instance, apart from attentively listening to their words, you will also observe their emotional experiences. Gauge how they are feeling based on what you hear (words), what you see (facial expressions and body language), as well as what you know to be true (intuition).

An example would be an employee who shares their frustrations working alongside a coworker. Even though you may not feel the same way about the coworker, you know how annoying it is to be misunderstood or treated with disrespect. Your intuition is what lets you know this information without having to experience the same situation yourself.

You can acknowledge the speaker's feelings by using validating phrases like:

- I know it isn't easy to share this information.

- Thank you for trusting me with this information.

- I can imagine what you are going through.

- I have been there before, and I'm sorry you are going through it.

- That sounds very stressful.

- I hear you and respect your opinion.

- Your thoughts and feelings are valid.

- It sounds like you need more support in this area.

- I know how challenging working in teams can be.

What is important to note about these phrases is that they don't necessarily state that what the speaker is saying is right or wrong. They are simply validating the speaker's reality. This, in turn, would make the speaker feel seen and heard.

Ask Empathic Questions

As a leader, you don't always need to have the solutions to employee problems or concerns. At the end of the day, you are also human and may not always understand or have the capacity to bring closure to a situation. Nonetheless, instead of shutting down or giving a dismissive response like "Well, I don't know what to do," you can ask empathic questions to continue the dialogue and gather more information about the employee's circumstance. With more information, you may be able to offer guidance on the suitable next step.

Here are examples of empathic questions:

- You seem preoccupied today. Is everything alright?

- How did you feel when that happened?

- How is this crisis affecting your performance right now?

- In what ways can I support you?

- Could you share more about what happened?

- How are you protecting your well-being in this situation?

- What do you think we should do about this?

- How can we work together to resolve this conflict?

Empathic questions should be open-ended to allow the speaker to reflect and provide a meaningful response. There aren't any wrong or right answers to empathic questions, so whatever responses you get, be open to investigating and testing them out.

Leave Your Assumptions at the Door

An assumption is a perspective drawn without facts or evidence. They can be harmless, like assuming there is enough paper in the printer, or serious enough to cause misunderstandings between people.

You make plenty of assumptions in a day, whether you are conscious of it or not. This is because, biologically, your brain creates mental shortcuts to conserve energy and speed up the time of decision-making. This means that when there isn't sufficient information available at the time of decision-making, you will make an assumption in order to take action.

Besides the shortcut taken by your brain, some of your assumptions can also stem from adopted beliefs and biases. For instance, you might assume that confident employees are more trustworthy than shy employees based on your understanding of confidence and extraversion/introversion.

Or you might believe that top-performing employees have high job satisfaction and poorly-performing employees have low job satisfaction, based on how you associate work ethic with employee engagement. These assumptions are dangerous because they can lead to unfounded judgments about employees that later change how you view and relate to them.

You can catch yourself making assumptions by paying attention to off-the-cuff remarks, such as:

- This is the way we have always done things.
- Interns can't be trusted.
- They will never go for that.
- Those ideas will never work here.
- If it isn't broken, why fix it?
- You don't know what you are talking about.
- People like them always cause problems.
- They will never listen to me.
- If someone has an issue with me, they will approach me.

Unchallenged assumptions can cause problems at work because, in many cases, they create an unrealistic—and inherently negative—depiction of reality. You and your team may have difficulty understanding each other or working toward shared goals because of unmet and unspoken expectations or suppressed anger caused by negative assumptions. Over time, these assumptions can grow and lead to divisions within the team, a lack of creative problem-solving, and low productivity.

If you are determined to challenge your assumptions, below are a few tips that can help:

1. **Ask for clarity**

It is difficult to stop yourself from taking mental shortcuts; however, you can learn to stop and ask clarifying questions about how you interpret what is happening. For example, a manager might assume that an employee is intentionally acting in ways that might sabotage the team by not responding to emails.

Instead of running with this assumption, they might call the employee aside and say, "When you don't respond to emails timeously, it makes me believe that you are attempting to slow down the productivity of the team. Is this true?" The benefit of this type of question is that it first allows the manager to create enough space in their mind for their assumption to be challenged, plus it gives the employee an opportunity to share their perspective.

2. Separate facts from opinions

In order to perceive something correctly, it must match reality. This means that thoughts based on facts are more likely to be true than thoughts based on opinions. When you assess the facts, there is little room for error in judgment. You have enough evidence to prove that what you are seeing is real. On the other hand, thoughts based on opinions can be laced with emotion and paint a picture of reality that is false. A simple question you can ask yourself before committing to a thought is: *What are the facts?* If you can find enough facts to back your assumptions, then the thought can be trusted.

For example, if you catch yourself thinking, "That employee is lazy," you can ask: *What are the facts?* If you are able to give sufficient evidence, such as not reaching targets, submitting poorly executed work, and frequent absenteeism, then there is enough proof that what you are thinking is true. However, if the only proof you have is that you don't like their attitude or you don't feel they participate in team discussions, then you must conclude that the thought is an opinion and cannot be trusted.

3. Be aware of your own projections

An important interpersonal skill to learn as a leader is being aware of your projections. We can define projections as unwanted thoughts or feelings that are pushed onto somebody else. Projects can make you think that someone else is living out the negative beliefs or behaviors you struggle to make sense of.

An example of a projection would be thinking that an employee who is quiet is holding secrets because of being betrayed by a quiet person in the past. Another example would be thinking that an employee of a different ethnicity is disrespecting you by expressing their concerns because of your past experiences being harassed by people of the same ethnicity.

One of the ways to manage projections is to be mindful of how your past experiences impact your relationships with others. Consider how some of the hurt you have experienced in the past has made it difficult to relate to people. Whenever you are interacting with others, remind yourself that they are unique human beings, who think and feel differently from you. Their reality does not match your reality; therefore, you cannot assume you know their intentions.

If you are unsure whether you are projecting or not, ask yourself: *What is mine, and what is theirs?* For example, if there is tension between you and an employee, get curious about where the tension is coming from. Could it be somewhat due to your own frustrations? Or is it something you feel coming from the other person? Take ownership of the unwanted thoughts and emotions you bring into a situation, which could be muddying how you view what is happening.

In Summary

Each individual has their own interpretation of what is happening around them. How you perceive a situation may not be how your employee perceives it. Instead of forcing them to adopt your worldview, you can show curiosity about learning how they see the world. Empathy is one of the tools you can use to make your employees feel seen and heard. Practicing empathy requires you to observe and reflect on another person's experience and imagine what they may be thinking or feeling. This kind of focus and attention given to employees can make them feel comfortable sharing their thoughts and feelings with you.

Chapter Seven

How to Find Like-Minded People

The successful networkers I know, the ones receiving tons of referrals and feeling truly happy about themselves, continually put the other person's needs ahead of their own. –Bob Burg

Making Connections Outside of the Office

Up until this point in the book, we have taken an in-depth look at the relationship between a leader and his or her employees. But we know that a leader's influence extends beyond the office. Of course, it is important for you to prioritize relationships with your team. However, to support the growth of the company and build a recognizable name for yourself, you will need to make time for networking.

There is a tendency for business leaders to think that networking is indulgent or optional. Those who share this view will typically decline invites to industry events, conferences, or social mixers. The mistake they make is to think that networking has no significance in helping them achieve their career goals.

The truth is that networking is a strenuous process that requires a great deal of investment to get right. The earlier you start building your network, the better. The closest thing I can compare networking to is buying stocks. The day you buy shares in a company won't be the happiest day of your life—but wait 5–10 years, and you will see a return on your investment!

Nobody starts out good at networking, except if they have exceptional social skills. The rest of us need to be trained on how to introduce ourselves to people, whom to invite into our network, and how to nurture those relationships.

The first step in making connections outside of the office is to familiarize yourself with the various types of "networks" you can create, such as:

1. **Operational network**

    An operational network consists of professional people who assist you in running your business and completing work tasks. These might include your employees, managers, suppliers, contractors, and agents. Like most leaders, you will have an operational network by default; however, you can strengthen your network by connecting with highly skilled talent and experts in your field.

2. **Personal network**

    A personal network consists of like-minded professional people who can offer support on your career journey. They don't necessarily help you make money, but being associated with them can boost your confidence, encourage personal development, and give you access to opportunities for coaching and mentorship. Examples of people who might be included in this network are colleagues, friends and professors from university, online coaches, and peers within industry groups.

3. **Strategic network**

    The third type of network is a strategic network, which consists of professional people who are experts in specific industry areas and can share skills, knowledge, and the latest industry information with you. Some of these people may also hold strategic positions of power within their organizations and can therefore draw your attention to potential business opportunities. People in this type of network include CEOs, managing directors, heads of departments, and members of industry associations.

Having built and nurtured these three networks, you could potentially gain the following benefits:

- **Be one of the first to learn about business opportunities:** When you are constantly engaging with business leaders or participating in industry conferences, you have access to the latest trends in the industry and can be one of the first companies to take advantage of opportunities that are presented.

- **Strengthen your internal team:** What you learn about business from engaging with experts can help you make workplace upgrades and improvements, such as restructuring your teams for more efficiency, improving your work culture, and being an overall better leader.

- **Gain access to a wider pool of talent:** There is no doubt that you have an excellent team helping you achieve company goals. However, the bigger your company gets, the more diverse skill sets and expertise you will need. Growing your network can help you connect with and recruit the best talent in the industry.

- **Be exposed to innovative ideas:** Since leaders are responsible for creating a vision and conceptualizing the future of the company, they need to connect with people who are creative thinkers and innovators. Some of the most creative ideas may not even come from professionals within your industry. It could be people from different fields who have a radically different business outlook from you.

- **Achieve business objectives:** Another practical benefit of having a network is being able to find someone with the right skills to get things done as soon as possible. For example, your team may not consist of a website designer, but this could be a skill that someone in your operational network has. Or perhaps you need international suppliers who can produce quality products so you can decrease costs.

Whether you are starting your business or have been around for a while, networks matter. To gain more influence, you will need to expand your strategic network and sharpen your networking skills.

Get In Front of Powerful People and Make Powerful Associations

It is quite normal for successful people to gravitate toward other successful people because they have similar interests, work schedules, and lifestyles. However, when you are intentionally growing your strategic network, these types of encounters cannot be casual.

When connecting with other leaders online or in person, your purpose should be to make powerful associations that are mutually beneficial and can offer long-lasting value. Don't be so quick to judge this tactic as manipulative. Remember, people do business with people they *like*, not necessarily people who are skilled or have the best operational systems. This means that the future of your company rests on strategic networks with other influential business leaders who have developed trust with you over time.

Getting in front of powerful people won't be easy. Just think about how many events you have missed because of work or how inconsistent you have been at creating a social media presence over the years. The same struggles are faced by other leaders. Even though they want to get out there and meet like-minded peers, they don't have time or are inconsistent at best.

What this means is that your approach in meeting and connecting with these folk will need to be more deliberate than attending an industry event or requesting a "follow" on LinkedIn. Below are a few strategies that can increase your chances of networking with influential people:1.

1. **Do your research**
   Ideally, you should always do research on the influential person you would like to connect with before the day arrives. The value of doing research is that you get to learn more about their professional career,

identify mutual connections (if there are any), get and get to know their interests and hobbies (this will help you strike conversations apart from business). The convenience of this digital age allows you to simply type a person's name in the search bar, and a series of articles and links tagged with their name will appear.

2. **Come recommended (if possible)**
Since we are still talking about ideals, another strategy to meet a powerful person is to come recommended. A mutual connection would be the one to approach the influential individual, make a brief introduction on your behalf, and set up a meeting or share your contact details. The reason why this strategy is so effective is that you can leverage the mutual's likability to establish your own relationship with the powerful person.

3. **Be loud about your similarities**
When you get your one-on-one time with the other person, it should be obvious to both of you why the meeting had to occur. Why? Because both of you have so much in common and are heading in the same direction. There is no way a powerful person can know how similar you both are without seeing some sort of indication.
To make the similarities loud without literally ranting about them, you can do things like wearing similar brands as them, talking in the same tone and style, sharing similar jokes, and showing passion for the same values and interests they have. If you don't know them personally, doing your research will help you learn more about what you have in common.

4. **Have something to give**
The irony of networking with powerful people is that you need to give more than you expect to receive. A powerful person may be skeptical of you if you are quick to ask for favors. When you do this, it sends a signal that you have nothing to offer in return, thereby making the connection transactional and only profitable for one person. Plus, influential people are so used to doing favors for others that they rarely connect with people who can add value to their lives. When approaching the powerful individual, have something to offer. Capitalize on things you are aware they are lacking, such as skills, insights, affiliations, or time!

5. **Ask and follow up**

    Eventually, you will have built a degree of trust that enables you to ask for favors. You have every right to ask for favors from your network, especially when you have generously invested your time, money, and expertise in helping them achieve their goals. When making your requests, be specific about how the other person can help you. This makes what you are asking for sound realistic and achievable (i.e., they will be more motivated to say yes). You should also plan to follow up with the individual if they don't respond with an answer.

Techniques to Gain Social Influence

Social influence refers to the ability to cause others to change their thoughts, feelings, or behaviors when interacting with you. It is a common skill learned and practiced by salesmen, advertisers, as well as businessmen for the primary task of selling. Nonetheless, the techniques of social influence can also be applied when networking and wanting to make a positive impression in front of others.

There are three societal norms that are internalized by human beings when they are still children and inform how they interact with others. These are the norms of duty, responsibility, and compliance. When unsure of the best action to take, people will most likely resort to these norms. Social influence techniques are based on the understanding and leveraging of these norms in order to influence another person's behaviors.

Below are examples of common techniques used to influence others and how to apply them:

Create an Illusion of Scarcity

It is an old adage that people want what they cannot have or access. In consumer psychology, scarcity is used as one of the ways to increase demand. You may have noticed advertisements with the captions "Limited time offer" or "Only a few spots left!" These ads are created to pressure customers to make a reactive buying decision. Even if they were not interested in the product, the fact that it might be taken away creates a desire for it.

How to apply: In the networking world, you can create an illusion of scarcity by maintaining exclusivity. Create boundaries that limit others' access to your time. For example, avoid lengthy meetings that go over 25 minutes as a way to show the value you place on your time. Choose a specific time of day when you answer or return calls and ignore calls that come in outside of that slot. Another trick is to be selective about the social networking events you attend and how frequently others get to interact with you.

Create an Air of Authority

We are conditioned as children to respect authority figures, whether it is our parents, school teachers, or the government. This respect causes many people to trust what authority figures say and follow their advice or instructions blindly. Subconsciously, we desire the approval of these authority figures to feel like we are responsible and compliant citizens.

How to apply: Create an air of authority about you. Since you are already a leader, this won't be a difficult thing to do. Identify certain skills and knowledge that you have acquired over the years which make you somewhat of an expert in that domain. Thereafter, look for speaking gigs, create a blog, or shoot videos of yourself sharing those skills. The aim is to slowly make yourself appear as a thought leader in the minds of your network; someone whom they can trust to share wisdom and information. If you haven't mastered any skills, now would be a perfect time to upskill yourself!

Create Win-Win Contexts

People understand that there is strength in numbers. As such, when you present an opportunity for them to partner with you on a project, as opposed to sponsoring your project, you are more likely to get their approval. Remember, nobody wants to feel left out of the ever-evolving business world. They want to be a part of the change, even if that means the only contribution they can make is offering their time or money.

How to apply: Whenever you are making a request to someone, present the request as an opportunity for them to collaborate with you. Explain what their role or contribution would be to the project and how much impact that would make. By the end of your pitch, the person should feel as though they were given a once-in-a-lifetime opportunity (creating an illusion scarcity) to make a difference.

Show Recognition

An unconscious desire people have is the need for social approval. As discussed in chapter 1, it matters to us what others think or feel about us. We are more likely to view relationships that offer validation as being positive and trustworthy than those that don't. Leaders who are sensitive to recognition can easily feel slighted when they are not given honor for their achievements. This might, in turn, make them behave unfavorably to those people from whom they felt rejection.

How to apply: Contrary to what many believe, showing recognition is a sign of strength and maturity, not weakness. Don't miss opportunities to show members of your network recognition. This could be as simple as leaving praise under a social media post where they talk about their achievements or being present to celebrate with them. Showing recognition also eliminates the air of competitiveness that is often created when two powerful people interact; instead of seeing you as a threat, they might see you more as a friend.

Model Positive Behavior

People can be influenced through social learning by watching the behaviors of others. This means that the best way to promote a specific behavior is to act it out rather than speak about it. The more evidence others see of the behavior working, the easier it is for them to start behaving in the same way. Naturally, people want to become the best version of themselves—it is an evolutionary need they cannot escape from. When they observe behavior that is positive and could potentially make them smarter, stronger, and more successful, they are more willing to adopt that behavior.

How to apply: Model the positive behavior you desire for others to demonstrate toward you. For example, if you would like people to be generous toward you, look for ways to demonstrate generosity. Give your time, money, skills, and knowledge whenever you have an opportunity. Make generosity a big part of your interaction with others, and watch how they gradually start behaving toward you!

In Summary

Networking is an essential part of personal growth as a leader. Not only does it give you access to people, skills, and opportunities that can level up your business, but it can also be a great confidence booster. There are three types of professional networks that you can work on strengthening at any time. If your goal is to gain more influence, then focus your energies on nurturing the strategic network. Get in front of powerful people, but make sure you don't come empty-handed. If you desire others to support and show up for you, you need to be the first to give!

Chapter Eight

Build Your Personal Brand

Your brand is your public identity, what you're trusted for. And for your brand to endure, it has to be tested, redefined, managed, and expanded as markets evolve. Brands either learn or disappear. –Lisa Gansky

Positive Self-Image and Effective Leadership

What separates leaders isn't so much their competencies as it is their personalities. Having managed teams for many years, leaders generally have the same skills and knowledge. But their leadership styles will look like night and day, depending on who they are.

Before you can think about the impression employees have of you, it's crucial to get clear on who you are. This message was emphasized earlier on in the book, too, because of how integral it is in building a positive self-image and gaining influence. To earn respect, for example, you must see yourself as a respectable person. And to be known as a confident leader, you must start by cultivating confidence from within.

The mistake that many leaders make is thinking that their position automatically earns them a good reputation. However, this isn't the case. Those leaders who go on to become influential have done the inner work of figuring out who they are and what value they can offer others. The reason they become influential is due to believing so much in themselves that all stakeholders are obliged to believe in them too.

A positive self-image goes hand-in-hand with success and opportunity. When you are confident in who you are, you have the courage to share your vision, take calculated risks, and enter boardrooms with a strong conviction. Because you have earned this confidence, you don't need to act overly aggressive or stereotypical of a "boss." People respect and form relationships with the real you—not your representative.

If your self-image has been muddied by past failures and insecurities, you can improve it by working on your personal brand. Your personal brand is the perception that others hold in their mind when they think about you. It is closely tied to self-image because when you trust and have full confidence in yourself, others will naturally sense that and offer you the same trust and confidence in return. However, when you are dealing with internal conflict, the same kind of confusion or mixed emotions will be mirrored in your relationships. This chapter will explore ways of improving your self-image by strengthening your personal brand.

What Is Your Personal Brand?

Imagine job-seekers reading a story about you or coming across your products inside a store and thinking to themselves, "I would love to work for this man or woman." Or potential customers watching an interview you recently did and being inspired to support your business. This type of influence is what leaders' dreams are made of!

The good news is that you can have that kind of effect on the people you work with or serve, but you will need to significantly improve your personal brand. There are a few myths about personal branding that need to be busted before taking the steps to establish yourself. These include myths like:

- **"Building a personal brand will make you successful overnight."** There are no guarantees that once you have established your brand, all of your problems will be solved. While a positive public perception is helpful in attracting business, there are many more factors that will ultimately determine if you succeed or not.

- **"Once you build a personal brand, you don't need to do anything else."** A personal brand requires regular maintenance. Your network will want to frequently hear from you after you have opened the lines of communication. This doesn't need to cost you a lot of money, though. It requires you to be consistent in sharing content, maintaining your distinct "brand voice," and keeping an honest public image.

- **"A personal brand is simply you being yourself."** There is some truth to this myth in the sense that authenticity is what allows people to form meaningful relationships with you. However, building a personal brand needs strategic thinking. Not only do you need to carefully select what you want your brand to be associated with, but you must also decide on the best way to convey your messages for maximum impact.

When you think of the most recognizable brands in the world of business, who do you think of? What are some of the ways in which those people have differentiated their brands from other leaders' brands? Even though their brands look and feel natural, you can be certain that millions of dollars have been spent on strategizing, implementing, and maintaining their brands.

Take the billionaire investor Warren Buffett, for example. How would any of us have known how successful he has been in the stock market industry if articles and books weren't created about him? Or how would he have earned the reputation of being frugal but philanthropic if we weren't informed about his charity work and The Giving Pledge (which he founded with Bill Gates), where he pledged to give away at least half of his wealth to worthy causes? (Valle, 2021).

Or what about Oprah Winfrey, who has been dubbed the "Queen of Media?" Without skillful personal branding, how would The Oprah Winfrey Show, named after the talk show host, have grown to become the highest-rated TV show in history? There wasn't much difference between her show and other talk shows, except for the fact that there is only one Oprah Winfrey, who exudes a special kind of authenticity and warmth that only she knew how to do.

Therefore, when establishing your personal brand, remember that you are unique, and while there are hundreds of competitors in your industry, no one can lead the way you do! Your personal brand won't become influential overnight, but with time people will come to associate certain thoughts, emotions, and experiences with you.

Simple Ways to Solidify Your Personal Brand

When solidifying your personal brand, you won't just focus on improving one aspect of your public persona but a collection of different things. Think of your personal brand as the summary of everything you stand for and hope to achieve, packaged in an email, social media post, or PR interview.

You will need to think about how you behave in the workplace, address employees, resolve conflicts, interact with customers, or navigate networking events. As police officers often state: Everything you do or say can and will be used against you! Below are a few steps that will help you begin the process of solidifying your brand. Feel free to conduct research or look for role models who can help you conceptualize your brand.

Step 1: Identify Your Brand Assets

Your brand assets are the toolbox of skills, knowledge, strengths, and beliefs that you possess that can help you stand out from the crowd. These brand assets will become the foundation of your personal brand—what people come to love and respect about you.

Write a list of your brand assets, focusing on the following categories:

1. Skills and credentials: What skills, credentials, and accomplishments have you obtained throughout your life?

2. Personality: What are some of the personality traits that make you

unique?

3. Core values and beliefs: What are some of your core business values and beliefs? What are some of the things you stand for and against?

4. Passions and interests: What subjects, ideas, and industries fascinate you the most? What are some of the things you are passionate about?

5. Purpose: What is your deep-rooted "why" for advancing your career? What are the desires you hope to achieve?

Step 2: Choose a Target Audience

The reality is that your personal brand won't appeal to everyone. For instance, there will be some people who aren't interested in the products you produce or the services you have to offer. It is, therefore, important to find a select group of people who might be inspired by your brand.

Think about graduates who have just left university and entering the workforce, suppliers who are interested in making new partnerships, or business leaders who are always looking to connect with other successful business people. Create a profile for your target audience, and explore what they like or dislike, what their career goals are, and some of the needs or challenges you can respond to.

Step 3: Create an Irresistible Offer

In order to maintain strong networks, you must have something valuable to offer your audience. Think about the value you want to associate with your brand. For instance, you might teach your audience specific skills, share knowledge through books or online courses, sell physical products, or offer coaching. Write your suggestions below:

Whatever your offer is, make sure that it solves a specific problem for your audience and helps them achieve specific results.

Step 4: Create a Content Strategy

Content is the physical or digital material that you create to share with others. Creating content is one of the best ways to sustain relationships with your network. Every now and again, they get to hear from you and are reminded of who you are and what you stand for.

Your content strategy must focus on certain topics that you are passionate about and that your audience finds interesting. To make things easy, choose between two to four topics that you want to be associated with. For example, if you are in finance, you might create content around investments, money management, debt management, and the psychology of money.

Brainstorm a number of different subtopics under those main genres and create a variety of articles, videos, podcasts, slideshows, tutorials, infographics, or webinars (depending on your preferred tools).

Step 5: Create a Visibility Strategy

The final step is to leverage other people's personal brands and audiences to get your name out there. A visibility strategy is all about getting exposure through strategic associations with industry experts, popular media channels, and relevant industry events.

Here are four ways to increase your visibility:

- **Guest blogging:** Write a feature article on a well-known blogging site or magazine that your audience reads.

- **Public speaking:** Deliver a talk at a local college, conference, or industry group that your audience attends.

- **Interviews:** Get interviewed by a podcaster, TV station, radio show, journalist, or publication that your audience also reads, listens to, or watches.

- **Partnerships:** Collaborate with other professionals and produce content or work on an offering (product or service) that would be appealing to both of your audiences.

Write down a few more examples of how you can increase your visibility.

These steps will help you build a brand that appeals to the right people, who are more likely to respond positively to what you have to offer. The key is to leverage online channels like social media to drive your messages forward and keep the dialogue between you and your network going.

How to Align Your Personal Brand With Your Company Brand

The risk of building a recognizable brand or being the face of your company is that what you do or say can heavily influence the decision to support your business or not. We have seen countless examples of business leaders whose businesses were negatively impacted by their chaotic private lives leaking on papers or their offensive language being caught on camera. These are extreme cases; however, in reality, it doesn't take these drastic inconsistencies to sabotage your business.

Being aware of how much is on the line, it is important to ensure that your personal brand aligns with your company's brand. In fact, if you have built the company brand first, you can use it as a benchmark for acceptable and unacceptable behaviors. Below are a few tips that will help you create a personal brand that is an extension of your company:

1. **Align yourself with your company values**
    Revisit chapter 4 and reflect on your company values. Can you remember why they mattered so much to you? Your company values are not only meant to be the blueprint for how employees perform at work but also a blueprint that informs your leadership style.
    Remember, employees will likely look to you for confirmation of the company values. When they see you living them out, they will have a greater sense of respect and appreciation for them too. Plus, you will notice consistency in how teams and individuals make decisions, solve problems, and interact with each other across the organization.

2. **Match your leadership style with your company culture**
    Your leadership style must match the atmosphere and values of your workplace. Imagine having an autocratic leader operate in a relaxed and hands-off type of culture. How confusing would that be for the employees? They wouldn't know whether to follow the boss's rules or create their own schedules and structures.
    Below is a table with five different types of leadership styles. Go through

the table and identify the style that best represents your company. Follow up by doing your own research about the style and how it would respond to various work situations.

3. **Ask for regular feedback**
The final tip to align your personal brand to your company's brand is to regularly ask employees to provide feedback on your leadership. This is a great way to learn what you are doing right and which areas you could improve. You can ask for feedback in a group session, on a one-on-one basis, or through a survey. The responses can be public or private, depending on how you would like to structure them.
Be open to receiving various kinds of comments, including criticism that may be difficult to accept. Remind yourself of the purpose behind the feedback session, which is to gather insights on how you can improve your personal brand.

In Summary

Building a personal brand can help you establish a reputation within your company and industry. Whether this reputation is positive or negative depends on how you portray who you are in the workplace and on public platforms. You have full control over your self-image and what you choose to associate with your brand. Be mindful of how you curate your brand, and ensure you represent the same values and culture of your business.

Part 3: Magnetic Presentations

Grab the Attention of Audiences, and Keep It

Chapter Nine

Techniques to Persuade Customers

Approach each customer with the idea of helping him or her to solve a problem or achieve a goal, not of selling a product or service.
–Brian Tracy

Identify Customer Pain Points

According to John Gottman, it takes five positive interactions to get over a single negative interaction (Benson, 2017). This has to do with the human brain's tendency to overestimate and feel more strongly about negative stimuli than positive stimuli. The question you may be asking yourself is if human beings are sensitive to negativity, where does that leave your customers?

Customers are the lifeline of your business. As long as you have a constant wave of customers supporting your business, your doors will remain open. You might remember that the way you found customers was to first identify a gap in the market—some kind of problem or unmet need. Essentially, what you were doing is looking for something negative that you can use to sell your products or services.

I remember shopping in a grocery store and walking past a poster advertising slimming tea. Holding the box of tea was a young, model-like woman with an hourglass figure. Right next to this goddess of a woman was the caption: *A cup a day will keep the bulge away!* The caption, alongside the image of the skinny woman, was designed to provoke overweight women to the point of feeling compelled to purchase a box of tea and manage their bulge. I thought the caption was harsh (to say the least), but it needed to be harsh in order to trigger a pain point.

Pain points can be defined as persistent issues that inconvenience customers. They get in the way of them living a healthy, productive, and responsible life. One might say, "If pain points are such a problem, why do customers spend so much time thinking about them?" The answer is that they provide negative stimuli, and anything that provides negative stimuli is overestimated in the human mind.

Businesses have made trillions of dollars by identifying and responding to customer pain points. Take the global beauty industry, for example, which is valued at $571 billion. What drives the sales of personal grooming products and cosmetics are unrealistic beauty standards, such as the desire to reverse aging, remove imperfections, or achieve facial symmetry. When the standard of beauty is so high, insecurities are created. Those insecurities become pain points that motivate customers to purchase the latest beauty products.

As a business leader, your revenue is determined by how well you can convince customers that they have a problem and that your products or services are the solutions they have been consciously or unconsciously looking for. You cannot rely on them to always understand their pain points because many consumers are unaware. You will need to conduct extensive market research on your target audience to familiarize yourself with their pain points.

Below are examples of customer pain points:

- **Productivity pain points:** Productivity pain points are problems that cause inconveniences. For instance, long queues at a grocery store, poorly built products, and manual processes are just a few examples of situations that waste a customer's time.

- **Support pain points:** Support pain points are caused by inefficient customer service. For instance, customers may not be able to get in touch with sales assistants during the buying process, or they may not get valuable support when expressing concerns.

- **Financial pain points:** Financial pain points occur when a customer isn't provided with sufficient information about the cost of goods or when they believe that the products or services are overpriced. The more a customer needs to do their own math and calculate how much the total purchase will cost (and if it is worth it), the less likely they are to go through with the sale.

- **Peer-related pain points:** Peer-related pain points refer to problems that manifest due to a customer's need to conform to social norms. This pressure is often created and spread through media by friends, family, and influential people. For instance, a customer might decide to make a purchase because of feeling left out, lonely, overweight, insecure, etc.

- **Growth-related pain points:** Growth-related pain points occur when a customer is motivated to transform the way they live. Unlike peer-related pain points, the motivation is not due to the desire to conform but instead to become a better version of themselves. For instance, a customer may decide to purchase an online course as part of their efforts to advance in their career.

A good tip to practice when researching customer pain points is to think about your buying process. Ask yourself questions like, "What encourages or discourages me from buying a product or service?" Explore the various conscious and unconscious considerations you make, such as price, process, and desire. It is likely that your customers are making the same deliberations before purchasing your products or services.

Techniques to Turn a "No" Into a "Yes"

In my late twenties, I had a mentor who told me that if I wanted to succeed in the world of business, I had to desensitize myself to the word "no." "You see, son," he said, "the word 'no' is an invitation to start a different conversation." He was right.

Hearing the word "no" didn't mean that it was time to pack up and head to the next potential customer. It was an opportunity to empathize with the customer's objections and see the challenges they might be exposed to.

In chapter 3, we spoke about the art of selling without selling and what to avoid when making a sales pitch. In this section, we are going to go one step further and discuss two effective techniques to turn a customer's "no" into a "yes."

Before you stop reading, I guarantee that these techniques do not require force or manipulation. However, you will need to present yourself as an expert on the product or service and speak with a sense of authority.

The sales business isn't for the faint-hearted because you will be rejected more frequently than you are approved. However, in the midst of rejection, how you respond is crucial to positively turning the situation around. The challenger model and cognitive dissonance are two techniques that can help you achieve this. Below is an in-depth look into both techniques and how to apply them.

The Challenger Sales Model

The challenger sales model is a sales technique that encourages you to find a successful "challenger" or high-performing sales rep that you can emulate when persuading a customer to follow through with a sale. However, even more than this, it presents an opportunity for you to demonstrate a sense of power and confidence.

A typical sales pitch follows a sequence like this:

Sales rep: Hello, am I talking to Mrs. Susan Dupree?

Customer: Yes, this is Susan. How may I help you?

Sales rep: My name is Ryan, and I am calling from Wireless Connections. I can see on my system that you are currently on our 500 Mbps home fiber plan. We are currently running a limited-time special on our 1 Gig home fiber plan that offers the fastest speed for smart homes like yours. Can I help you switch today?

Customer: No, thank you. I am comfortable with my current plan.

Sales rep: But with our current special, you will continue to pay the same rate for six months, while enjoying the perks of high-speed internet. Don't you want the cost benefits?

Customer: No. I am satisfied with my plan right now. I will reach out to you when I am ready to upgrade. Thank you for your time.

At this stage of the conversation, the sales rep usually doesn't know what to do besides drop the call and cross the customer off his long list of leads. If they were using the challenger model, this wouldn't be the end of the conversation. In fact, it would be the beginning of a different kind of conversation; one where they show the customer how much value they are potentially missing out on and why they need to change their minds.

This is done through three steps, known as the "T-T-T." Below is an overview of each step.

Teach the Prospect the Value of the Product

You can make a positive assumption that the reason the prospect is saying "no" is because they are skeptical or lack knowledge about the product. Tell yourself, "This 'no' comes from a place of ignorance, and by educating them about it, they might change their mind."

It will be difficult to educate a prospect on a product that you know very little about, so before attempting to teach them anything, make sure that you know what you are talking about. Create a cheat sheet with the main points about the product, such as the name, origin, various uses and benefits, and a few how-tos. The focus of your pitch should be on answering the whys: Why should I care? Why is it beneficial for me? Why must I buy it now?

Tailor the Message to Suit Your Prospect

If you are working on a list of leads, chances are the prospect is already a member of your target audience. However, just because they fit the target audience profile doesn't mean they are interested in the product you are selling. For instance, they may be interested in purchasing a product but have a few constraints that are standing in their way, like not being able to afford the product or having other priorities that take more importance in their life.

This is when truly empathizing with your customer can be a game changer. Instead of taking their "no" as being final, ask questions to understand where they are coming from. Give them an opportunity to explain what challenges they are facing, so that you can tailor your message to be more accommodating to their needs. Show how your product or the promotion you are running can help to solve their specific problems.

Take Control of the Sales Process

At this point, the conversation is leaning more toward your favor. If you have been successful at breaking down the barriers that were causing your customer to object, then you are able to accelerate the sale and encourage them to take action. It is important to pay attention to your message at this point because the customer can still change their mind. Avoid sounding apologetic or creating options. Be clear when defining the steps your customer will need to take to move the sale forward. Acting quickly and swiftly will work in your favor as long as you have provided satisfactory solutions for all of your customer's concerns.

Using the same script as above, here is a version applying the challenger model:

Sales rep: Hello, am I talking to Mrs. Susan Dupree?

Customer: Yes, this is Susan. How may I help you?

Sales rep: My name is Ryan, and I am calling from Wireless Connections. I can see on my system that you are currently on our 500 Mbps home fiber plan. We are currently running a limited-time special on our 1 Gig home fiber plan that offers the fastest speed for smart homes like yours. Can I help you switch today?

Customer: No thank you. I am comfortable with my current plan.

Sales rep: But with our current special, you will continue to pay the same rate for six months while enjoying the perks of high-speed internet. Don't you want the cost benefits?

Customer: No. I am satisfied with my plan right now. I will reach out to you when I am ready to upgrade. Thank you for your time.

Sales rep: I understand, Mrs. Dupree; however, may I ask if you work from home?

Customer: Yes, I do.

Sales rep: And do you have children in their pre-teen or teen years?

Customer: Yes, I have two teenage boys.

Sales rep: What if I told you, Mrs. Dupree, that you can host hour-long video conferences while one of your boys plays online video games and another downloads movies without experiencing any buffering, failed downloads, or poor-quality video calls?

Customer: That would be wonderful!

Sales rep: Our 1 Gig home fiber plan is our bestselling plan for a good reason. Many of our customers have families and often struggle with Wi-Fi issues due to having so many devices connected. With faster internet, the whole family can be connected at the same time without experiencing any lags or seeing frozen screens.

Customer: Okay, that makes sense. So, how does the upgrading process work?

From here on out, the sales rep would rehearse a script and define clear action steps the customer would need to take to move the sale along.

Leveraging Cognitive Dissonance

Customers can be held back from purchasing products because of something called cognitive dissonance, where a person holds two contrasting beliefs or feelings toward something. For example, you might desire fast food but at the same time question yourself because you know it is unhealthy. A purchasing decision will be made depending on which belief is strongly reinforced in your mind.

The example above highlights the inner conflict between what is perceived as "good" and "bad." Ironically, there are many companies that sell products or services that are seen as being both good and bad. Cigarette manufacturers know that their customers deal with inner conflict each time they think about purchasing a packet of cigarettes. What makes this even worse is that by law, manufacturers are forced to add warning labels about the health risks of smoking on every packet.

Imagine how much deliberation the marketing teams of those manufacturing companies undertake to create marketing campaigns that break through the cognitive dissonance. A notable cigarette brand that succeeded in changing the narrative about cigarettes is Marlboro.

During the 1950s, when cigarette smoking was publicly shunned by the medical community, they created a fictional character called the "Marlboro Man," who was depicted in adverts smoking a cigarette whenever he did manly tasks like fixing a car or riding a horse. The sense of self-assuredness and independence he exuded was what every American man desired for themselves at the time. The campaign was so successful that afterward, Marlboro became one of the largest global cigarette brands.

What products or services do you sell? Do they cause cognitive dissonance in customers' minds? Below are a few strategies that can help you leverage cognitive dissonance to turn a "no" into a "yes."

Appeal to the Most Favorable Belief

Get familiar with the conflicting beliefs your customers have about your products or services. Focus your sales and marketing efforts on appealing to the favorable belief (the one that works in your favor). Seek to play up this belief and provide as many reasons why your customer is justified to think that way.

For example, if you are selling a high-quality product that comes with a high price tag. Find reasons to make the customer believe the product is worth the cost. Mention positive attributes about the product, such as the quality materials, which can cause them to justify the purchase in their mind.

Use the Opposite Tone

This strategy works when customers are more likely to hesitate when purchasing your products or services. Perhaps you are in an industry that is still seen as a social taboo, like gambling, or maybe your product is seen as indulgent, unhealthy, or unproductive. To break through cognitive dissonance, you can use the opposite tone. For example, if customers are more likely to think negatively, your campaign can be upbeat and positive.

Include Relevant Facts

Another way to break through cognitive dissonance is to provide more information about the product or service. It is possible that customers have misconceptions about your offerings or their uses, and some relevant facts can be enough to persuade them. For example, car manufacturers tend to include relevant facts about their latest car models to show consumers what they are getting and how this particular model differs from the previous ones.

In Summary

A customer pain point is a problem that either gets in the way of them making a sale or encourages them to seek after certain products or services. You can use pain points as an incentive to connect with customers and make tailored pitches. Plus, techniques like the challenger model and cognitive dissonance present opportunities for you to explain how your offerings can solve their problems.

Chapter Ten

What's Your Follow-Up?

There is no magic to closing. There are no magic phrases. Closing the deal is completely dependent on the situation. –Alice Heiman

Find Ways to Keep the Conversation Going

It is very rare for someone to buy a product or service upon hearing about it for the first time. In marketing, the rule of 7 states that a customer must be exposed to a message seven times before they feel confident to take action.

Moreover, a study by Brevet showed that 80% of sales require reps to follow up five times before closing a deal. In contrast, only 44% of sales reps make a single follow-up before giving up (Williams, 2020). What this means for your business is that the first sales pitch may not be sufficient to close a deal. You may need to follow up with them on several occasions to make them feel comfortable making a transaction.

A sales follow-up describes the process of reaching out to a potential or existing customer and encouraging them to take action or provide feedback. This type of engagement can be done through different channels, but the two most common are telephonically and via email.

The reason why many sales reps dislike the follow-up process is that they don't necessarily know what to say or how to make it valuable for the customer. As a result, when following up, they might use meaningless phrases like:

- *I was just checking in about last week's call.*
- *I wanted to find out if you got my email.*
- *I was curious to know if you have made a decision yet.*
- *I haven't heard back from you. Are you still interested?*

The fact that the prospect is answering the phone or reading emails should be a good indication that they are still interested. Instead of coming across as pushy, desperate, or aggressive, your follow-up must add some type of value. Below are some suggestions to consider:

- **Make a connection.** Start the conversation by mentioning a significant moment or piece of information learned from your previous call or email. For example, you can ask about their kids or a new product they have recently launched, depending on what you both spoke about.

- **Guide the conversation back to the prospect's pain points.** It is important to make their pain points the focus of the follow-up because what you are essentially selling them is the solution. Plus, if they are still experiencing the same problems, they won't mind receiving more information on how to fix them.

- **Include engaging content.** Inserting links to articles, videos, or promotions can add value to your follow-up. Subconsciously, it makes them feel obligated to return the favor by giving you something, too (which, in your case, is making a purchase).

There are two important stages of the sales process when making follow-ups is ideal. The first is after initial contact has been made with the prospect. Instead of re-introducing yourself, you can pick up where you left off. Go over the value of partnering with the business and the benefits of purchasing the product or service. Essentially, you are reminding the prospect of the "good parts" of your previous call or email.

Here is an example of a conversation or email you might send:

Hello Sylvia,

It was a pleasure introducing our business to you over the phone.

I have been thinking more about how we can save you time by integrating our software into your current work processes.

I thought you would be interested to learn how our software has helped Client A and Client B automate 60% of their work tasks.

Follow the link below to watch the video:

[add link to video]

I hope you have found the video helpful.

I would like to schedule a 10-minute call with you to share more details about the features our software comes with. Are you available next week Wednesday or Thursday?

Propose the Next Steps

It is important to take control of the sales process until you have closed the deal. While getting a prospect to say yes over the phone is a positive step, it doesn't mean much if they haven't committed to taking action. Throughout your engagements with the prospect, you should keep the end goal in mind. In other words, be intentional about moving them along the awareness, consideration, and decision-making stages.

Proposing the next steps doesn't need to be a significant request, like getting your prospect to make the final decision over the phone. It can simply be a small action that can keep the conversation between you flowing, such as:

- Asking for a 10-minute Zoom meeting.
- Asking to connect on LinkedIn.
- Asking if you can make a sales presentation.
- Asking if you can add them to your mailing list.
- Asking to send more information about your product or service.

During a call, you can propose the next steps by asking a yes or no question. An example of this would be:

Mr. Kumar,

I enjoyed our chat today. I was wondering if you are free next week to have a 10-minute Zoom meeting with our Sales Director, who will take you through the demo of our software?

The next steps can also be proposed after a sale has been made. What's good about these "next steps" is that they can be automated and sent as part of your email sequence. Examples of the kind of next steps you can send include tracking of shipment, requests for product or service feedback, additional product recommendations, or offering a small gift to thank the customer.

Ask for Feedback

After making a successful sale, you can follow up by asking for customer feedback. Feedback is important to gauge how satisfied customers are with the buying process and which areas you may need to improve. What customers have to say about you can also give prospective customers an indication of what they can expect when doing business with you. Positive feedback can be repurposed and used as part of your pitch when persuading prospective customers.

There are plenty of ways to ask for feedback without coming across as pushy. If you are not comfortable requesting feedback in person or over the phone, you can request it via email, social media, on receipts or invoices, or on your website. You can also decide on the type of feedback to ask for, like switching between customer service, product quality, or buying process feedback. It all depends on what you are trying to measure at the time.

There is no guarantee that customers will provide feedback after making a purchase, but the more ways you make the request, the more willing they will be to take action. Here are a few creative ways to ask for feedback:

Thank You Cards

If you sell products or services in a physical store, you can print out thank you cards that every customer gets to go home with (attached to the receipt). On the card, you can type out something simple like:

> *Thank You!*
>
> *From all of us here at Cupcake Boutique, we would like to say thank you.*
>
> *If you have enjoyed your experience, please leave a review.*
>
> *Simply scan the QR-code below:*

Order Confirmation Email

A great way to ask for feedback if you own an online store is to insert a few lines requesting a review as part of the order confirmation email. What makes this method effective is that the buying process isn't entirely complete (the customer is waiting for their goods), and they are more likely to still be engaged. Plus, this would be a good time to ask for their feedback on the buying process since it is still fresh on their mind. The feedback sentence can be structured like this:

> *Thank you for shopping with us at Cupcake Boutique! Tell us about your shopping experience by leaving a review on our website [insert link to website].*

Direct Emails

When asking for reviews from formal stakeholders like business partners or suppliers, you can send a direct email. The likelihood of them responding favorably to the request is higher in comparison to asking customers because you may have built more personal relationships with these stakeholders. Even though you are familiar with them, ensure that the email is still formal. You can send a message similar to the one below:

> *Dear Mr. Larson,*
>
> *Thank you for an awesome collaboration on this project. We couldn't have done it without the expertise of your talented staff.*
>
> *Would you be willing to share your experience working with us on our LinkedIn page?*

Social Media Surveys

Another way to reach out to customers and ask for feedback is by creating a feedback survey and posting a link on social media. The only risk with this strategy is that you might attract people who aren't real customers and simply want to sabotage your feedback results. Perhaps as a tool to filter out fake customers from real ones, you can ask respondents to provide their most recent order or invoice number as a form of validation. The following simple caption can accompany the link to your survey:

> *We love hearing from our customers. Please show us some love by completing a short survey [insert link].*

To increase your conversion rate, make the process of giving feedback as simple and quick as possible. Reduce the steps involved and questions asked to encourage customers to follow through. Take the time to respond to feedback, whether good or bad, as a way to acknowledge and show appreciation to your customers.

In Summary

It is your job to guide each customer through the sales journey until you have closed the deal. In most cases, this will involve following up with a prospective customer several times and taking them through the next steps. To avoid coming across as pushy or desperate, make each engagement valuable. Ditch the generic follow-up phrases and tailor your message to the specific customer you are talking to. Finally, once the sale has been made, don't be shy to ask for feedback. This will give you an indication of what you are doing right and areas where you can improve.

Chapter Eleven

What You Can Learn From Steve Jobs

Designing a presentation without an audience in mind is like writing a love letter and addressing it 'to whom it may concern. –Ken Haemer

Public Speaking Lessons From a Billionaire Hippie

When you think of prolific speakers of our time, Steve Jobs certainly makes the list. However, this eccentric and soft-spoken man wasn't born with the talent for speaking. According to Steve Wozniak, the friend, and co-founder of Apple, Jobs was not the best computer engineer, so he had to be the "face" of Apple and learn how to sell their products.

What I appreciate about Steve Jobs' story is that it shows other business leaders that communication skills can be learned and mastered. You don't need to be born with a special gift to engage audiences to become one of the best speakers in the world. All you need is the desire to learn how to convey messages that impact listeners.

So, what lessons can we learn from Mr. Jobs about effective public speaking? After watching a few of his recorded speeches and analyzing what he did or said that made his presentation powerful, I came up with four factors that every aspiring public speaker should learn: storytelling, emotional connection, memorability, and preparation.

Lesson 1: Tell a Story

Product launches are not typically theatrical events. The CEO or Marketing Director will stand on stage and address a crowd of employees, members of the press, and a few influencers. His or her speech will start by giving context to how the product was conceptualized, followed by an explanation of the features and a short demonstration.

That's it. Product launch done and dusted.

But Steve Jobs had something different in mind. Whenever he stood upon stage, his intention was to tell a story. The reason for this is that he knew the best way to influence people is to get them to buy into the purpose or "why." With audiences invested, he could then proceed by selling the product.

Like any good story, Jobs began by introducing the hero and villain. In his case, the hero was Apple and the villain was whichever company or ideology that was seen as a threat to the progression of his vision. His speech would be structured into three stages: the setup, confrontation, and resolution.

During the setup, Jobs would paint a picture of the conflict between the hero and the villain; the confrontation would describe the tension between innovation and tradition and the kinds of challenges the hero would be up against. Finally, the resolution would bring the story full circle and show how the hero was able to win against all odds.

Below are a few excerpts from his speech at the Macintosh pre-launch in 1983. As you go through the speech, see if you can identify the hero and villain, as well as the transitions between the three stages (i.e., setup, confrontation, resolution) (S, 2018):

It is 1958. IBM passes up the chance to buy a young fledgling company that has invented a new technology called xerography. Two years later, Xerox is born, and IBM has been kicking themselves ever since.

It is 10 years later the late sixties Digital Equipment DEC and others invent the mini-computer. IBM dismisses the minicomputer as too small to do serious computing and, therefore, unimportant to their business. DEC grows to become a multi-hundred million dollar corporation before IBM finally enters the mini-computer market.

It is now 10 years later the late seventies, in 1977, Apple, a young fledgling company on the west coast, invents the Apple II, the first personal computer as we know it today. IBM dismisses the personal computer as too small to do serious computing and unimportant to their business.

The early eighties '81, Apple II, has become the world's most popular computer, and Apple has grown to a $300 million dollar company, becoming the fastest growing corporation in American business history with over 50 competitors vying for a share.

IBM enters the personal computer market in November '81 with the IBM PC. 1983 Apple and IBM emerged as the industry's strongest competitors, each selling approximately one billion dollars worth of personal computers in 1983; each will invest greater than fifty million dollars for R&D and another fifty million dollars for television advertising in 1984, totaling almost one-quarter of a billion dollars combined, the shakeout is in full swing.

It is now 1984; it appears IBM wants it all. Apple is perceived to be the only hope to offer IBM a run for its money; dealers initially welcoming IBM with open arms now fear an IBM-dominated and controlled future. They are increasingly and desperately turning back to Apple as the only force that can ensure their future freedom.

IBM wants it all and is aiming its guns at its last obstacle to industry control. Apple, will big blue dominate the entire computer industry? The entire information age? Was George Orwell right about 1984? Our enemies shall talk themselves to death, and we will bury them with their own confusion. We shall prevail! On January 24, Apple Computer will introduce Macintosh, and you'll see why 1984 won't be like 1984.

Lesson 2: Establish an Emotional Connection

It worked in Steve Jobs' favor not to have grown up being a good speaker. This is because whenever he spoke, there was some kind of rawness (perceived as authenticity) in his speech. He wasn't afraid to change his tone and pitch throughout the speech to emphasize different points and show his passion. And when the message called for it, he would express emotion and reveal a more vulnerable side to himself.

It mattered more to Jobs that he connected to audiences more than selling information or products. He did this by leveraging different kinds of public speaking techniques. For example, even though he wasn't known to be funny, he would insert some humor into his presentation to lighten the mood or poke at one of his competitors. Or if he was speaking about a touching subject, like his health issues, he understood the power of the pause.

The secret to creating an emotional connection with audiences was in his delivery of the speech or presentation. Jobs knew that his demeanor on stage and how he delivered the message would influence how audiences responded. He focused on a number of details that would make him appear more open, friendly, and relatable.

For instance, his outfits were mostly all black and bland to shift the audience's focus on his actual speech. He spoke in a casual and relaxed demeanor, as though he was telling a few friends what he had been up to over the past few months. He also knew how to carefully craft his message and had a preference for clean presentation slides with a few but potent adjectives and visuals. All of these tactics helped to create a mood in the room and kept audiences engaged from the beginning until the end.

To understand how Steve Jobs used emotional language to connect with listeners, here is an excerpt from a Commencement Ceremony speech he gave in 2005 at Stanford University. In the speech, he bares all by openly speaking about his losses and experience coming to terms with his medical diagnosis, which he links back to the transitional season of life the graduates are in, and offers words of encouragement to help them through this exciting but terrifying life stage (Studocu, 2017):

When I was 17, I read a quote that went something like: "If you live each day as if it was your last, someday you'll most certainly be right." It made an impression on me, and since then, for the past 33 years, I have looked in the mirror every morning and asked myself: "If today were the last day of my life, would I want to do what I am about to do today?" And whenever the answer has been "No" for too many days in a row, I know I need to change something.

Remembering that I'll be dead soon is the most important tool I've ever encountered to help me make the big choices in life. Because almost everything is all external expectations, all pride, all fear of embarrassment or failure - these things just fall away in the face of death, leaving only what is truly important. Remembering that you are going to die is the best way I know to avoid the trap of thinking you have something to lose. You are already naked. There is no reason not to follow your heart.

Lesson 3: Make the Speech Memorable

Consumers are faced with hundreds of brand messages each day. In order to ensure that your messages stay top of mind, it is important to make them memorable. Introducing your business the traditional way and presenting information that audiences can easily find online won't make your presentation memorable. By the time you are done talking, the audience will have forgotten what you said.

Steve Jobs wanted Apple users to think about his products everywhere they went. To own so much space in the user's mind, he needed to find ways of making his ads and speeches memorable. There are two distinct ways in which he did this. The first was to deliberately add a shock factor, something that the audience didn't expect would create a positive feeling. In some speeches, this was done through video and, in others, through provocative language. The second thing he did was to include visual elements in the form of symbols or icons that made it easier for audiences to remember what he spoke about.

One of his most memorable speeches was about the launch of the iPod in 2001. Apple had invited the media to the launch, as was the tradition, but nobody knew what product was going to be unveiled. The element of surprise added a hint of drama and anticipation, which was a great tactic to get everybody intrigued.

Jobs began his speech by making an emotional connection with the audience (Guglielmo, 2021):

We love music, and it's always good to do something you love. Music's a part of everyone's life -- everyone. Music's been around forever. It will always be around. This is not a speculative market. And because it's a part of everyone's life, it's a very large target market all around the world. It knows no boundaries.

He then proceeded by telling the hero and villain story, where Apple was the tech innovator who was entering the digital music player industry and seeking to bring change, and the existing companies in the industry were the villains who were selling outdated and clunky devices.

What made this particular speech memorable was how he described the iPod. It would have been enough for Jobs to introduce it as a portable digital music player since that would be the first of its kind. However, he went a step further than that and described it using a catchy phrase: 1,000 songs in your pocket. This metaphor helped users visualize what owning an iPod would be like since they had never been able to carry around their CD players before. Moreover, he went into detail explaining the specifications of the iPod and its many features to show the return on investment (Guglielmo, 2021):

If we're going to keep 1,000 songs on an iPod and it fits in your pocket, how do we do this? How do we possibly do this?

We start off with an ultra-thin hard drive. We've got a 1.8-inch diameter hard drive that's 0.2 inches thick -- super thin. And that hard drive is five gigabytes in capacity -- 5 gigabytes -- which holds 1,000 songs at a 160-kilobit rate, which is a very high quality rate of MP3 compression.

Very high quality. 1,000 songs on this 5-gigabyte drive. And we built in 20-minute skip protection. That's not 20 seconds -- 20-minute skip protection, so you can take iPod bicycling, mountain climbing, jogging, you name it, and you're not going to skip a beat.

I highly doubt that users remembered every spec mentioned by Steve Jobs on that day; however, what they walked away with was the excitement of being able to store 1,000 songs in their pockets. A simple catchphrase was all Jobs needed to dominate the digital music player market.

Lesson 4: Don't Ignore the Preparation

Delivery is a crucial part of any presentation. What often persuades people to listen isn't so much what is said but how it is said. Steve Jobs was known to rehearse his presentations countless times, weeks before the actual day. His speeches would run for more than an hour long, but not once would he read notes because of the amount of preparation he did in advance.

Since he wasn't a natural public speaker, he couldn't leave his preparation to the last minute. Many business leaders have wondered what Jobs' preparation process entails, but a few years ago, Ken Kocienda, a principal software engineer who worked on building the original iPhone, gave insight into how Steve Jobs prepared for his keynote addresses. Below are some of the main points (Gallo, 2018):

- Jobs would start to rehearse written portions of his speech about three to four weeks before the actual day. He would practice at the venue with the proper stage lighting and presentation that would be shown on the day. He would go over whatever material he had rather than waiting until his speech was complete.

- Jobs would memorize everything pertaining to his presentation, from each line of his speech (and what it meant for him and the audience) to the structure and content of each slide. Like a theater production director, he enjoyed conceptualizing how everything would come together on the day and how each person present in the room would connect to the presentation.

- Most of Steve Jobs' power was in his delivery. He spent countless hours refining his tone of voice, pace, pitch, and style of communication. Even though he looked cool, calm, and collected on stage, his energy, gestures, and demeanor were intentional.

- Before the day, Jobs would perform his speech in front of his executive team and ask for feedback. He specifically wanted to know how he could improve his slides or phrase certain words or sentences better.

In his book titled *Creative Selection*, Kocienda made the following observation about Jobs, "As needed, [Jobs] stopped, stepped out of character, reduced the volume of his voice, and asked executives seated in the front row what they thought of some turn of phrase or whether they believed the ideas flowed together smoothly" (Kocienda, 2019). After receiving feedback, Jobs would take a short pause, get back into character, and continue practicing his speech.

In Summary

You don't need to have a natural talent for public speaking to develop the skill. With the right intentions and discipline, you can learn how to prepare speeches that tell stories and keep audiences captivated. The techniques used by Steve Jobs were not invented by him; he simply studied human behavior and put together various tactics to create an emotional appeal and persuade people to listen to him. You have the ability to have the same kind of influence on your listeners, but not without extensive public speaking training.

Chapter Twelve

A Crash Course on Public Speaking

The mediocre teacher tells. The good teacher explains. The superior teacher demonstrates. The great teacher inspires. –William Arthur Ward

3 Principles of Public Speaking

If you want to trace back the origin of public speaking, you would need to go as far as ancient Greece, where it is believed to have begun. Citizens in ancient Greek used public speaking to persuade and praise each other when suggesting or opposing laws in their assemblies (Spencer, 2021).

Centuries later, when Rome came into power, the same tool was used during the political discourse. Most of the teachers who taught public speaking in Rome were of Greek descent, and this style of communication continued until the mid-20th century. After World War 2, a Latin style of public speaking became popular in the US and Europe. Instead of the formal and political Greek style of public speaking, society leaders adopted a conversational style of speaking.

The fact that there are styles of public speaking should tell you that public speaking is, to some extent, an art form. The reason why it is an art is because there are so many ways of getting it wrong and few ways to get it right. If you think back to the speeches or pitches you have sat through at work or private functions, you will notice that very few (if any) are memorable. The fact is, it doesn't take much skill to make a speech. What's difficult is grabbing the audience's attention and keeping them engaged throughout the speech.

As a business leader, you will be given many opportunities to stand in front of people and introduce your business or sell a product. While you are up there, your goal will be to convert doubters into believers and ensure that your presentation is unforgettable. Public speaking can help you package a message in a way that helps you connect with others and even entertain!

The following sections will explore three basic principles of public speaking that can enhance your communication and persuasive skills.

Don't Try to Be the Best

There is a tendency for us to think that we need to be perfect on stage. We admire the likes of Steve Jobs and dream of having the same effect he had. But from everything we have discussed in this book, we can safely say that seeking perfection isn't the route to authenticity.

The first principle of public speaking is to avoid being the best. This isn't an invitation to be mediocre but instead a call for you to feel comfortable being yourself. When you are standing at a podium with lights in your face and a crowd full of faces waiting to hear what you have to say, being yourself can help you speak with fewer nerves and more conviction.

Nobody else can play "you" as well as you can. Not even Tony Robbins or Gary Vaynerchuk. The competitive advantage you have when you are doing public speaking is that you can share your message with your authentic voice. Below are a few tips for helping you lean toward being yourself:

Tell a Personal Story

You have plenty of stories about losses and victories that have shaped your career journey. These stories make great analogies to give context to a topic or convince audiences of why what you are saying matters. Even if you are presenting a formal speech, telling a story can add a touch of authenticity to show audiences that your data is grounded in real-life experiences.

Here are a few ways to weave personal stories in your speech:

- Set the stage: "I remember five years ago when we launched our first product…"

- Explain the premise of the story: "For the first two years of our startup, we were operating at a deficit."

- Introduce the action: "Despite our cost-saving initiatives, our monthly revenue was staying the same. This got us thinking about how else we could scale our business."

- Explain outcomes and lessons learned: "After implementing the new software, we were able to achieve…"

Express Your Personality Through Your Attire

Public speakers use dressing as a tool to convey a certain message about who they are. This is a distinct way to share a bit about your personality and add some depth to your speech. Don't let anyone tell you that you need to wear a suit, unless of course that is part of your professional image. Dress in a manner that best represents your style, even if it means going against conventional norms.

Some of the iconic speakers of our time who have expressed themselves through dressing are:

- The signature black turtleneck and jeans was how Jobs arrived for every public address. It became a sort of uniform that helped audiences focus on his message rather than being distracted by what he was wearing.

- Researcher and author Brene Brown is known to wear casual jeans and a top whenever giving a talk. The simplicity of her dress complements her laid-back and down-to-earth personality.

- Entrepreneur and business coach, Dan Lok, is famous for wearing black ties and formal suits when giving a presentation. This outfit choice matches his sophisticated brand and has earned him the nickname "King of High Ticket Sales."

Don't Match Energy

One of the ways to tell the difference between an experienced public speaker and one who is starting out is to look at their energy on stage. Experienced public speakers have a way of owning the stage and infecting the audience with their charm and confidence. In contrast, speakers who are starting out have the tendency to match the audience's energy and let them determine the flow of their presentation.

The issue with the second approach is that when the audience is quiet or seems disengaged, it can throw the speaker off. They can also mistakenly interpret the lack of responsiveness as a sign of boredom. The truth is that the audience can only give back what they receive. In most cases, they are mirroring the kind of energy they sense from the speaker. Matching the audience's energy can be a big distraction and cause you to lose sight of your intended message and delivery.

To ensure that you own the stage, focus on the "why" behind your message. Become so wrapped up in the purpose of what you are saying that other people's perception of your message doesn't matter. Doing this may require self-awareness, such as noticing when you are nervous, fidgeting, or simply reading your notes without any emotion. Take a pause and channel the same attitude and energy that you started the speech with.

Know Your Audience

Whether you are addressing an audience of five or fifty, it is important to know who you are speaking to and what they expect to hear. You can spend weeks compiling a powerful presentation, but when it is given to an audience that cannot appreciate it, you won't achieve the desired outcomes.

For example, giving a talk about retirement planning to college students won't have the same impact as giving the talk to seasoned professionals who are more invested in this topic. There are three things to remember when analyzing your audience:

1. **Think about how your audience relates to the topic**
   When researching the topic of your presentation, think about why the topic matters to your audience. For instance, is it a particular pain point they wish to solve? Or can they learn something from this topic? If the topic reveals cognitive dissonance, consider the conflicting beliefs your audience may have about it.

2. **Consider how knowledgeable your audience is on the topic**
   Presenting a topic that is too advanced or simple for your audience can cause them to become disengaged. It is important to gauge how much your audience knows about the topic and whether the information you are presenting is appropriate or not. You can test this out by asking for feedback before the actual day to make sure you are offering enough value to keep the audience interested without confusing or boring them.

3. **Learn about the diversity of your audience**
   Nowadays, it is more common to find a diverse audience with a mix of people from different cultural backgrounds than one where everybody is the same. Thus, being mindful of the differences and how they might impact your message is key. If possible, ask someone whom you trust to read your speech and provide feedback. Remove ambiguous statements or jokes that might be seen as sarcastic or offensive.
   If you are fortunate enough to have a homogenous audience, where everyone has the same interests and personality, here is how you can adapt your presentation to suit their preferences:

Hostile audience

A hostile audience has high expectations of speakers. They are used to listening to people they know and like, and may be quick to judge new speakers or those who they perceive as being uninformed. In a business context, a hostile audience can also be a group of angry consumers or competitors who dislike your organization. Instead of being hostile toward them, here are a few ways to engage:

- **If possible, seek to prove your credibility.** Realize that they may not trust you yet, but at least they can respect the fact that you are a legitimate business or competent business leader who knows what they are talking about.

- **Find ways to agree with some of their beliefs.** A hostile audience will likely be "anti" everything that you value or stand for. Finding common ground can help you bridge the gap between you and forge a connection. Study their beliefs and find commonalities that you can present in your speech. Link them back to your argument and take a firm standpoint.

The aim is not to treat the hostile audience with animosity, as this may reaffirm what they think about you. Instead, be courteous and base everything you say on data and facts. Create very little opportunity for them to find loopholes in your argument, regardless of whether they agree or disagree.

Uninformed audience

You may think that an uninformed audience is ideal because you can swoop in and teach them something. But in actual fact, they can be a difficult crowd to navigate! Unlike the hostile audience, this group doesn't have an attitude problem, but they have a really big knowledge gap—so big that you may not be able to bridge the gap in one presentation. This can backfire because, in the absence of information, the uninformed audience will make assumptions, further widening the knowledge gap. When presenting to this audience, remember the following:

- **Start the presentation by asking questions.** This is a great way to see how much the audience understands from the get-go. Encourage them to shout out keywords or present their opinion about a topic. Refer to their responses throughout the conversation to connect your message with their level of understanding.

- **Keep your presentation simple.** The worst thing you can do to an uninformed audience is overload them with information. Keep your slide minimal (more visuals than text) and use language that they can understand.

Don't make it your goal to teach an uninformed audience everything. Focus on reinforcing a single idea or theme, then leave the rest for the follow-up presentation.

Sympathetic audience

A sympathetic audience is the easiest to influence because they are open, compassionate, and willing to learn. Even if it is your first time presenting to them, they will make you feel welcome by showing responsiveness and being polite. Nevertheless, just like any other audience, they have expectations too. What they desire most is to form an emotional connection through your message. Here is how you can achieve that:

- **Tell personal stories that reveal your human side.** Don't worry if you go off-topic; this type of audience doesn't mind learning personal details about you.

- **Use emotive language that can strike a chord with the audience.** For example, when speaking about your business losses, use the words "failure," "setback," or "painful moment." When speaking about your successes, mention the words "achievement," "growth," and "blessing." These words are layered with meaning and can cause the audience members to reflect on their own life experiences.

The trick to winning with a sympathetic audience is to show vulnerability. They will be able to see right through any inauthenticity or a desperate attempt to connect. You don't need to offload your entire life story on stage, but make sure you deliver the message with sincerity.

Practice Your Delivery

The idea of delivering a speech or presentation sounds straightforward—simply read what you wrote down, or try your best to not look down at your notes. However, in reality, the delivery is about having a moment with the audience. A lot of time and preparation goes into presenting an engaging speech. While the speaker may look natural and confident, I can bet that they are conscious of what they say, how they say it, and every transition of their presentation.

Effective public speaking isn't solely about verbal communication. It also takes into consideration non-verbal communication, the venue, the distance between the speaker and the audience, presentation slides, sound and lighting, and so on. Therefore, from now onward, when you think about the delivery of your presentation, bear in mind that it refers to the awareness of your internal and external environment and how that interacts with your message.

There are four methods to structure your delivery. Please note that you don't need to follow any of these methods rigidly; they can be used as a guide when planning how to deliver your speech or presentation. The four methods include:

Impromptu Speaking

Impromptu speaking often occurs during special occasions like birthdays when you are asked to stand up and say a few words about the host or at a networking event when you are asked to briefly introduce yourself. What distinguishes this type of delivery from others is that it is usually a short and heartfelt message that comes from the top of your mind. No prior preparation is taken before the time of delivery, so you are unable to anticipate what you will say. At best, impromptu speaking can make you appear genuine and at worst, it can be humiliating!

Before you start speaking, take a few seconds to repeat the question to yourself and collect your thoughts. If possible, have at least one point or idea that you can expand on. For example, if you are asked to introduce yourself, have at least one idea you would like to emphasize, such as your role and experience as the CEO of a company. Keep your message brief to allow for a balanced back-and-forth conversation. Lastly, if you are going to use humor, make sure you are comfortable enough with the audience to handle negative feedback.

Extemporaneous Speaking

Most business leaders deliver speeches or presentations using extemporaneous speaking. With this approach, the aim is to deliver a rehearsed speech in a conversational manner, with little reliance on notes. You intentionally create an atmosphere where the audience feels like they are listening to a good friend. As such, they are more relaxed and willing to learn from you.

Another unique element of this method is the constant assessing whether the audience is following and buying into your message. This can be done by naturally surveying the room with your eyes and determining how responsive the audience is. If audience members seem disengaged, you will know that there is something about your delivery that is lacking. Perhaps the issue has to do with your monotone voice, the ratio of facts to storytelling, lack of humor, or not enough gestures. Either way, you can swiftly adjust your approach and reassess the audience's response.

Manuscript Speaking

There are a few business leaders who practice manuscript speaking, where the objective is to deliver a speech by reading the manuscript word-for-word. This method is most common among political leaders; however, when you are presenting a business report, company policy or legal contract, or data-dense market research, it is more appropriate to read than trying to memorize the script. However, since the focus is solely on reading properly, it is important to enunciate your words and read with vocal expression. When practicing your delivery, find a few videos of news reporters and politicians, and take a few tips on how they engage listeners with their voices.

Memorized Speaking

Memorized speaking refers to rehearsing a speech or presentation to the extent of not relying on notes or slides (even though you may have them with you). For the entire duration of the speech, you utilize different parts of your body to connect with the audience, like maintaining eye contact, using your hands, raising your eyebrows, smiling, etc. While this is perhaps the most difficult method of delivery, it can be the most powerful when done right. Without the distraction of looking down at your notes, you have an opportunity to use your body and visual presentation as a tool to emphasize your message.

In Summary

Public speaking involves more than just talking to an audience. It is about sharing stories and impactful messages to hopefully connect and persuade an audience to take action. In order to have this kind of effect on people, you must study the audience you are speaking to, figure out the best way to deliver your message, then commit to being yourself on stage. Developing your public speaking skills takes a lot of practice, so demonstrate the discipline to do the necessary preparation.

Part 4: Magnetic Culture

Create an Environment That Brings Out the Best of Your Employees

Chapter Thirteen

Culture Starts With You

Become the kind of leader that people would follow voluntarily, even if you had no title or position. –Brian Tracy

What Type of Leader Do You Aspire to Be?

Imagine if you went undercover into your workplace, disguised as an intern, and to your surprise, discovered that your employees were dissatisfied with various aspects of the business. What kind of conversation would you have with them afterward?

The TV show, *Undercover Boss*, is based on this very concept. In each episode, executives from across the US pose as newly recruited entry-level workers for their organizations and spend a few days job-shadowing different employees. Under their disguise, they are able to get up close with employees and learn about their work experiences.

In one of the episodes, Larry O'Donnell, former COO of Waste Management, disguised himself as a new recruit and job-shadowed employees in several departments within the company. He learned that the push from headquarters that was meant to encourage workers was decreasing morale and causing low productivity. He was also informed about unjust disciplinary measures, like a two-minute pay cut for every minute late, and how these were also contributing to low morale.

This insight allowed O'Donnell to implement a few impactful changes. The first being that he would pay more attention to the needs and concerns of front-line workers and involve them in decision-making processes where they might be directly or indirectly affected. Over the following months, O'Donnell and the executive team noticed an improvement in employee morale and engagement (Fam, n.d.).

You don't need to masquerade as a fake intern to learn how employees perceive the work environment. All you need to do is look into a mirror and face yourself. Shows like Undercover Boss typically attract leaders who have very little self-awareness, to the extent that they need to be confronted by employees before they can make necessary changes. Just by understanding yourself and knowing your strengths and weaknesses, you can be more socially aware of the impact you make on others.

I have consulted with plenty of executives throughout my career, and almost all of them have been shocked whenever I break the news: Culture boils down to leadership. Unfortunately, hiring the best talent won't magically create a high-performing culture, nor will offering free pizza and beers on Fridays. The individual or group responsible for shaping and maintaining a work culture are the executives. They do this by modeling the values, attitudes, and behaviors that they desire to see at work.

Creating a dynamic work culture shouldn't be an afterthought. In fact, I recommend that leaders make it one of the agendas when refining the business strategy. You see, the level of satisfaction of workers has everything to do with the bottom-line. If employees aren't happy coming to work, they won't be motivated to perform. In the interim, you can work on becoming the type of leader that employees want to follow. Notice that I used the word "want" instead of "need," which indicates that they choose to respect you and adopt your vision as their own.

Five Levels of Leadership

What is common among leaders is that they have a growth mindset. This mindset is what helps them commit to continuous learning. I would even argue that without believing that they can better themselves, they wouldn't have reached their position in the first place.

The growth mindset also dictates that the leader's development is never finished. This is good news because it means that leaders always have room to improve. They are not the same leaders they were a few years ago and certainly don't come close to the leader they will be in the future.

Many leaders feel discouraged when they identify holes in their leadership. They become self-conscious and fear that they will never regain the trust of employees. For some reason, they forget that being a leader isn't about achieving perfection but rather committing to constant growth. In his book, *The 5 Levels of Leadership*, John Maxwell outlines five progressive levels that every leader will cross in their career (Maxwell, 2013). These levels demonstrate the evolution of a leader, going from someone who is given the title to someone who has earned it.

Below is a brief explanation of each level and how to move swiftly to the next one. As you go through the list, reflect on the level you are currently at and what it might take for you to graduate to the next one.

1. **Position**
   The "entry-level" of leadership is getting placed into a position of power. Getting here is not easy, and there is no doubt that you have the capabilities to perform your duties. Nonetheless, having the position doesn't earn you respect or trust. At this level, your team follows your lead because they need to, not necessarily because they want to. It is important to work on building meaningful relationships with your employees—with no strings attached—to begin developing a foundation of trust.

2. **Permission**
   The second level is where employees start to warm up to you and feel comfortable opening up. This is a good indication that you have invested

enough time into building and nurturing those relationships, and your hard work is starting to pay off. However, it becomes more critical to develop your social and communication skills, such as showing empathy, creating emotional safety, and communicating assertively. The more you actually like the people you are leading (and they like you, too), the more positive influence you can have over them.

3. **Production**
By level three, you have successfully earned the respect of your employees. You will notice that your engagements with them feel more natural and mutually beneficial. Moreover, you start seeing them as mentees, and they start to see you as a mentor. With this much influence, you can motivate your team to increase their performance without sounding pushy. If you play your cards right, you can bring positive change to your workplace. Just remember that you need to give twice as much positive reinforcement as what you expect out of your employees. This means that rewards and recognition should be common occurrences at your work.

4. **People Development**
Later on, when you have established systems and the company is running smoothly, you may want to step back from the business and focus on other interests. This is when you start to focus less on your personal development and more on the development of future leaders in your organization. Your time is spent on "reproducing yourself" by educating and training employees to follow in your footsteps. Even if retirement isn't on the horizon, you may want to upskill employees so they can meet the future expectations of the company.

5. **Pinnacle**
The final level is acquired after many years of serving as a leader. You reach the pinnacle of your leadership when you start to see the return on investment of all of the time, effort, and training you have put into developing people. Your positive reputation causes employees to compete to work with you or to be mentored by you. Directors from other companies may try to recruit you or at least request to consult with you.

Your association with the company attracts more customers, suppliers, and investors.

Note that the pinnacle isn't the end of your leadership journey. With the enormous amount of influence that you have, you can look for ways to continue expanding your impact. It is common for leaders who reach their pinnacle to become philanthropists, start leadership programs, write books, or become public speakers. You can decide how you want to commit to continuous learning and improvement!

Developing Emotional Intelligence

Emotional intelligence (EQ) can be defined as the ability to understand and regulate your emotions and respond empathetically to the emotional experience of others. This soft skill isn't a prerequisite for employees only, but for leaders too. When a leader demonstrates high emotional intelligence, they are able to show accountability, communicate better with employees and make decisions that are in the best interests of all stakeholders.

We always emphasize the importance of trust between employers and employees; however, rarely do we assess what it takes to build trust. You can think of EQ as one of the building blocks that help employers build trust with employees. This is due to being able to practice self-awareness and constantly evaluate how their actions impact those around them.

There are four components that you can work on to develop a higher EQ. These include improving your self-awareness, self-management, social awareness, and relationship management. Below are explanations of each component and questions to help you gain a deeper understanding.

Self-Awareness

Self-awareness is the ability to be conscious of your own thoughts and feelings. When this occurs, you are able to challenge your beliefs and emotions before acting upon them or holding them as truth. Self-awareness can be helpful in various workplace situations involving employees, particularly when conflict or misunderstandings ensue. You are able to separate your thoughts and feelings from the action taking place in real life or from what your employees are thinking and feeling.

Scenario: You notice that an employee's productivity has dropped, and they aren't meeting their usual targets. Your initial thought is that they are lazy and expect to be carried by the rest of the team. You take a moment to reflect and realize that this is your own projection. In your mind, low productivity is equivalent to laziness, but this may not be what's happening in real life. You decide to call a meeting to provide feedback and see how you can help the employee improve.

Here are a few reflection questions that you can answer to increase self-awareness:

1. What kinds of situations bring out the best in you? What do they have in common?

2. What kinds of situations bring out the worst in you? What do they have in common?

3. When you are feeling overwhelmed, what coping strategies help you maintain level-headedness?

4. What does it take to make you feel motivated?

5. How do you take constructive criticism? How might you improve?

6. What is your level of willingness to learn from others? How might you improve?

7. What type of employees do you naturally gravitate to? Describe what it is about them that you connect with.

8. What type of employees do you tend to avoid? Describe what it is about them that triggers you.

9. What beliefs are you holding that sometimes get in the way of leading your team? Where do these beliefs come from?

10. When these beliefs arise, what can you say to yourself to challenge them?

Self-Management

Self-management, also known as self-control, refers to the ability to remain resilient during stressful work situations. Your brain's natural response will be to either attack, disengage, or go into complete shock. However, neither of these strategies is useful, especially when your team is looking to you for guidance. Similar to self-awareness, self-management enables you to regulate thoughts and emotions; however, it goes a step further and helps you determine acceptable and unacceptable behaviors in different workplace contexts.

Scenario: During a meeting, an employee voices their concerns about a recent decision you made, but quickly loses their temper. Instead of speaking respectfully to you, they raise their voice, point fingers, and cause a scene. You feel the urge to raise your voice and assert dominance as the leader but decide to take a deep breath and empathize with what they might be feeling. You recognize that their frustration has very little to do with you per se and more to do with their interpretation of reality. You de-escalate the situation by validating their viewpoint and asking them to have a private conversation to speak about the matter.

Self-management is an incredibly difficult skill to master because of the level of discipline it requires. Nonetheless, with practice and reflection, you can learn to control your behaviors in a professional environment. Here are a few reflection questions to help you gauge your level of self-control:

1. What is your approach to managing your time at work?

2. What has been the most difficult part about managing your strong emotions at work? What coping strategies have proven to be effective?

3. What is your approach to resolving conflict between two coworkers? Describe the step-by-step process below:

4. What is your approach to resolving conflict between you and an employee? Describe the step-by-step process below:

5. How do you process personal failure, such as taking actions that nega-

tively impact your team?

6. How do you deal with mistakes or losses made by your employees?

7. What are your beliefs when it comes to sharing thoughts and emotions at work? What do you deem acceptable and unacceptable?

8. What are some of the workplace boundaries you have established to create a safe and healthy work environment?

9. Are there any behaviors that are prohibited at your workplace? If so, what are they, and why are they not allowed?

10. How do you hold yourself accountable as a leader? List at least five ways that you practice self-discipline.

Social Awareness

Social awareness is the ability to reflect on how others might be impacted by your actions and behaviors. Unlike self-awareness, where you are encouraged to look internally, social awareness promotes others-centeredness, being strongly motivated to protect the interests of others as much as your own. Bear in mind that you don't need to agree with what others think or feel to bring social harmony. You simply need to acknowledge that others might think or feel differently from you.

Scenario: You get feedback from employees that the current office work schedule isn't working. The majority of them feel that it would be better to implement a hybrid work schedule, where a few days are spent in the office and a few days at home. You aren't entirely satisfied with this arrangement, but instead of dismissing their suggestion, you decide to organize a meeting where you can get to understand where they are coming from and potentially find common ground.

Social awareness encourages you to step outside of your comfort zone and understand people better. Here are a few reflection questions to help you explore your degree of social awareness:

1. Describe a situation where you dealt with a difficult employee. How did

you handle the situation, and how might you improve in the future?

2. How do you know when an employee will be a good cultural fit for your organization? What are the qualities you look for?

3. Describe a time when an employee raised concerns about a decision you had made. How did you address their concerns, and how might you improve in the future?

4. What is your approach to improving employee engagement? List a few strategies that have proven effective in the past.

5. In what ways do you support employee growth and development? What are some of the initiatives you have put in place at work?

6. In your opinion, what are the common causes of misunderstandings in the workplace, and how do you address them?

7. Name at least one company value that is practiced most often at your office. Why do you think this value has been so successful?

8. Name at least one company value that is rarely practiced at your office. Why do you think employees have struggled with this value?

9. Describe a situation where changing your leadership style brought about positive changes at your work. What were some of the mistakes you were making and how did you rectify them?

10. Describe the typical mood or atmosphere within your team or organization. What are some of the norms or practices that help to maintain this energy?

Relationship Management

Relationship management is the ability to build and nurture workplace relationships through a variety of initiatives, such as effectively communicating ideas, setting healthy boundaries, creating channels for employees to share their thoughts and feelings, and fostering teamwork. What makes relationship management unique is the fact that it requires you to have strong EQ (i.e., having high self-awareness, self-management, and social awareness). Without it, you may find it difficult to manage workplace crises.

Scenario: The conflict between two members of your team has grown and is starting to affect other employees and their productivity. Since teamwork is vital for the success of your organization, you decide to call the two members aside to address the conflict. Seeing that there is no sign of resolution between them, you make the decision to place them into different teams and monitor their behaviors for the next month.

Relationship management is hard because you are human too, and sometimes can be biased. However, you can curb biases by focusing on acting in the best interests of the company. Here are a few reflection questions to help you gauge how good you are at managing workplace relationships:

1. Describe a time when you had to issue a written warning to an employee. What offense did they make, and why did it warrant a warning?

2. Describe a time when you were managing a team with employees who had very different personalities. How did this affect team performance, and what steps did you take to maintain steady productivity?

3. Give evidence that you have established a positive work environment for employees to work.

4. How have you improved your level of empathy over the years? What challenges have you overcome?

5. What type of behaviors do you still struggle to tolerate from employees? What steps can you take to improve tolerance?

6. Describe the most difficult boss you have had. What lessons about relationship management did you learn from them?

7. Describe a time when you failed to positively manage a relationship with an employee. What lessons can you take away from that experience?

8. Describe a time when you were shown appreciation or recognition from

an employee. What were they praising you for?

9. What new insights have you learned about managing people in the past year? Provide examples.

10. What traditional principles of relationship management do you believe are outdated or ineffective? What alternatives would you propose?

In Summary

Healthy and positive workplaces don't just happen. They are built by the efforts and intentions of the leadership team. You are responsible for shaping the kind of work environment you desire by modeling positive leadership. Your work culture will evolve at around the same pace as you evolve as a leader. You can positively influence your work culture and employees by committing to continuous growth and learning.

Chapter Fourteen

What Does a Positive Work Culture Look Like?

Culture isn't just one aspect of the game; it is the game. In the end, an organization is nothing more than the collective capacity of its people to create value. –Lou Gerstner

Work Culture Explained

To recruit the best talent and ensure you get the best out of them, you will need to build a great work culture. A work culture is simply the collection of values, attitudes, and practices that shape a work environment. Every organization has a culture, whether they have intentionally created one or not, but not all work cultures are positive spaces for employees.

It is difficult to describe what a positive work culture should look like since every company is built differently. For example, what might boost employee engagement in a results-driven workplace won't necessarily work in a coaching-driven or charismatic workplace. Nonetheless, there are a few elements that every positive work culture has in common, which are listed below:

1. **Accountability**

   In positive work cultures, every person working in the company, regardless of their titles or positions, is held accountable for their actions. The executive team follows the same rules, expectations, and disciplinary measures enforced on employees. They are also able to be questioned or challenged for their decisions and asked to account. This type of environment that fosters openness and transparency causes employees to feel seen and heard.

2. **Equity**

   Another element of positive work culture is that employees are treated fairly. Rewards and recognition are given based on merit, not classifications like age, race, ethnicity, gender, sexuality, or cultural background. These work environments are also more likely to promote diversity and inclusivity across the organizational hierarchy. Knowing that opportunities are accessible to anyone can be encouraging for employees who seek to advance their careers.

3. **Communication**

   Open and honest communication is encouraged in positive work cultures. Employees are given several communication channels and people to reach out to when seeking to offer feedback, share ideas or concerns, or discuss their goals and development. Freedom of expression is usually accompanied by open and honest communication, which allows employees to express their opinions and beliefs respectfully, even if they are at odds with company policies. There is no conversation that is off limits as long as thoughts and emotions are expressed with others in mind.

4. **Recognition**

   One of the main identifiers of a positive work culture is the amount of time and effort managers and leaders spend on recognizing and rewarding top-performing employees. Showing employees how much they are appreciated boosts their motivation and incentivizes them to continue working diligently. Recognition is also given in multiple ways, ranging from monetary benefits to public announcements and awards.

Some leaders take the risk of not crafting their work culture for themselves and instead allowing it to naturally take shape. The danger of doing it this way is that without expectations on how to interact with each other, employees will establish their own norms and values. In the worst-case scenario, unwanted beliefs and behaviors may become common in the workplace, which can create and spread toxicity.

The benefit of taking the extra time to create a positive work culture is that you control the energy at work and can predict how employees should respond in various work situations. Similar to a school environment, it is also easier to enforce discipline when rules or boundaries are violated. In the long run, the culture you create will reinforce itself as more employees learn to embrace and protect it.

6 Types of Positive Work Cultures

If you are managing or leading a startup company, you have the creative freedom to choose what kind of positive work culture you want to establish. However, if your company has been in existence for a while and perhaps has a recognizable culture already formed, you have less room to play around. You can, however, look at your current work culture and find ways to fine-tune it so that it can become the positive work culture you envision.

Here are three questions to consider when fine-tuning your work culture:

1. **What are the positive attributes of your culture that stay the same?**
   The benefit of having a solid culture is there are positive elements that have already been developed. Write a list of what these positive elements are, so that you can incorporate them into your new and improved culture. If you like, you can also have an open discussion with your employees and ask them what they appreciate about working at the company. Ask them to think of various aspects of their job and identify positive practices.

2. **What is the company's existing structure?**
   Your work culture should not deviate from your company structure. When this occurs, it can create confusion for teams and interfere with existing

work processes. When redesigning your work culture, make sure that it aligns with your hierarchical structure. For instance, traditional structures support and work best with traditional cultures, and modern, unconventional structures are complemented by modern, unconventional cultures.

3. **How do you currently interact with stakeholders?**
When redesigning your work culture, be mindful of how it might impact employees, customers, business partners, and other stakeholders. Positive improvements to existing practices will be welcome more openly than new practices that still need to be learned and adopted. To ensure that your stakeholders are on board with your plans to improve your work culture, consult with them before making any major decisions. Be open to hearing their thoughts and concerns and taking them into consideration.

After you have made up your mind to revamp your work culture, you will need to think about what a "positive work culture" looks like for your business. Below are six examples of positive work cultures and a list of pros and cons for implementing each one (O.C. Tanner, 2022):

Adhocracy Culture

An adhocracy prides itself on being innovative and taking risks. This type of culture appeals to tech companies like Apple or Facebook and is likely to attract highly skilled and creative employees who want to be a part of technological change. Teams within the organization are encouraged to solve problems using unconventional methods and continuously improve products and services.

Pro: Employees are encouraged to take ownership of their time and tasks. This enables them to create their own expectations and organize their time. Having limited restrictions on their creativity can enhance work quality and performance.

Con: Employees who are not self-driven and enjoy thinking outside of the box can find this type of workplace challenging to adapt to.

Clan Culture

A clan is a group of people that support one another in achieving common goals and interests. Companies with this type of work culture tend to function like a family and value teamwork. You will typically find family businesses or small mom-and-pop stores operating in this manner. Almost all company goals are achieved as a result of collaboration, and as a result, competition among employees is frowned upon.

Pro: Hierarchical structures don't really exist, or at least aren't emphasized, in these cultures. The environment is usually one of support and encouragement.

Con: Competitive, results-driven employees may feel that they don't have any room to grow in such a company.

Customer-Focused Culture

Customer-focused cultures place importance on customer service and satisfaction. Almost all of their processes are designed with the customers' convenience and happiness in mind. Examples of companies that have adopted this type of culture are Zappos and Amazon. These two companies show what lengths businesses will go to acquiring and retaining customers.

Pro: Customer-focused cultures will prioritize employee engagement because they recognize how instrumental employees are in keeping customers happy. Therefore, their work environment is likely to be positive and productive.

Con: When employee satisfaction is neglected, workers can feel underappreciated compared to the treatment customers get. This can start internal company politics and conflict, as seen with Amazon in recent years.

Hierarchy Culture

Traditional workplaces that promote a hierarchy culture can be positive too! While they are risk-averse and prefer sticking to the same set of rules that have carried the organization since its conception, these types of workplaces are organized and provide employees with a stable environment. Every employee knows what is expected of them and the processes they must follow. As long as the company is performing well, employees feel secure about their jobs and can focus on climbing the corporate ladder.

Pro: Employees are given the necessary resources and tools to succeed at their job.

Con: Innovative, risk-taking, or non-conforming employees may find this type of workplace too restrictive and unable to provide enough opportunities to grow.

Market-Driven Culture

In market-driven cultures, the focus is on becoming the dominant brand or business in the market. The best way to achieve this is to outperform competitors. Examples of companies that have adopted this type of culture include Tesla, Salesforce, or another business that can brag about being the "world's number one…" at performing certain activities. You will most likely find high-performing employees in these workplaces who pride themselves in meeting work expectations.

Pro: Employees have a lot of room to upskill themselves and advance their careers in these types of work environments because there is always an abundance of work to do.

Con: Employee satisfaction can take a backseat when performance is all that matters to the company.

Purpose-Driven Culture

Purpose-driven cultures are built on a strong purpose that informs work goals and processes and helps to keep employees motivated. Non-profit organizations and community-focused businesses tend to have this type of culture because it is their objective to rally stakeholders behind a cause. Employees who work for these organizations aren't necessarily looking to climb the corporate ladder; instead, they want to make a positive difference in the lives of others.

Pro: Purpose-driven workplaces tend to attract employees who are loyal to a cause and are more likely to stay at an organization, even when the conditions are unfavorable (i.e., not getting salary bonuses every year).

Con: Since these companies prioritize social impact more than being profitable, they can sometimes run into financial issues, making it harder for them to afford to recruit a great team.

In Summary

Every business has a work culture, but they may not be positive environments for employees. What makes a work culture positive is the willingness of the entire team to commit to practicing healthy and productive values, beliefs, and behaviors on a day-to-day basis. If you already have a work culture but desire to fine-tune it, consider positive elements that already exist, how your company is structured, and how you can improve interactions with your stakeholders. Remember to stay true to what you stand for as a business and create a culture that enhances your best qualities.

Chapter Fifteen

Get Out of Your Employees' Way

Micro-managing creativity kills it. To encourage creative brilliance, foster an atmosphere where it can thrive, and then step out of the way and let it happen. –Stewart Stafford

How Micromanaging Can Ruin Your Culture

The biggest threat to a positive work culture is micromanagement. We can define micromanagement as a style of management where excessive control is used. As a result, employees are unable to fulfill their duties to the best of their abilities.

Almost everyone has a story about working with a micromanager. My first experience with a micromanager occurred back in university days when I worked part-time as a barrister. Although, I'm not sure I can count this job as "work experience" because my manager never allowed me to do anything, let alone make coffee for customers.

He was everywhere at the same time, looking to see what every worker was up to—hoping that we weren't taking initiative and doing tasks without his knowledge. Before leaving the shop, like taking a lunch break, we had to report to him. And god forbid we took more time than what we had initially asked for. As you can imagine, it didn't take very long before I started looking for another part-time job.

A micromanager is an employee's worst nightmare because they slowly drain the life out of a team or department. Some micromanagers simply lack emotional intelligence and aren't able to assess how their behaviors impact those around them. While other micromanagers are aware of their behaviors but struggle to give up control.

It would be easy for us to judge micromanagers and pass them off as obsessive. However, to get behind this toxic workplace behavior and root it out of our organizations for good, we need to understand what causes micromanagement. Some of the reasons that lead managers to become controlling include:

- **Perfectionism:** Managers who impose excessively high standards for themselves will invariably impose the same high standards on their team. They might think to themselves, "If I can respond to emails past midnight, they can too."

- **Negative self-beliefs:** Similar to the point above, managers who have a negative self-concept and tend to speak to themselves critically may also see their employees through the same lenses. For instance, if they fear making mistakes because it is perceived as a sign of laziness, then this is also how they will address mistakes with employees.

- **Inability to trust employees:** Another potential reason for micromanagement is the lack of trust in the capabilities of employees. This could be an egotistical thing, such as thinking that nobody on the team has skills that can match their level or genuinely doubting the quality of work produced by employees.

- **Fear of conflict:** There are some managers who assume most of the responsibilities to avoid confrontation. For instance, if a team member is slacking, they will insist on completing their work for them (rather than calling them into order). This can be frustrating for an employee who desires to learn how to improve their skills or work performance.

- **Obsession with power:** Perhaps the most commonly cited reason for micromanagement is the obsession with power. Not every micromanager is motivated by power; however, those who are can treat their employees like subordinates. Any kind of task completed without their knowledge can be seen as an attempt to steal their spotlight or upstage them.

You can imagine how difficult it must be to work alongside a micromanager. Despite how amazing the work culture can be, having a controlling boss dampens an employee's spirits and affects their productivity. Your business will be indirectly impacted due to high employee turnover, little to no innovation, employee burnout and disengagement, and poor quality of work.

How to Prevent Micromanagement In the Workplace

As much as we would like to think that we are incapable of becoming micromanagers, it is easier than we might realize. Let's spend a few moments reflecting on the pressures of leadership from a newly appointed manager's perspective. Just imagine that you have recently been appointed as the manager of a department. While you may have earned this role, having this much authority over a team of employees is a new experience.

Let's assume that for more than five years, the only person you were responsible for managing was yourself. As a result, when you enforce work standards in your new role, you tend to assume that everyone structures their time and workflow the same way you do. Even if your intention isn't to stifle your employees' performance, the constant fear of jeopardizing your leadership career can cause you to obsess over the details.

Can you see how easy it is to fall into the trap of micromanaging? Fortunately, as a leader, you are able to root out micromanagement by simply training your managers to apply certain strategies when supervising their teams. These may include:

1. **Hire the right people**
One of the simplest ways to prevent micromanagement is to hire com-

petent people. Steve Jobs was famously quoted saying, "It doesn't make sense to hire smart people and tell them what to do; we hire smart people so they can tell us what to do" (Schwantes, 2019). When you have a highly skilled team, you can rest assured that they are capable of solving problems on their own and meeting targets without supervision.

2. **Manage expectations, not tasks**
When you have hired the best talent, you don't need to sweat the small stuff. How each employee decides to structure their time or complete tasks is up to them. Remember, you are working with experts, not rookies. To monitor progress, you can arrange weekly or bi-weekly check-ins to assess whether each person is on schedule to meet deadlines. These check-ins can also be used as feedback sessions and an opportunity to allow employees to ask questions and vice versa.

3. **Work in a separate space**
It might help to physically separate yourself from employees so that they feel a sense of autonomy. Of course, you will still be reachable for questions and feedback, but you won't constantly linger around them during work hours. Having a separate space can also help you shift the focus away from employees and to your own work tasks. As time goes on, you will feel less of an inclination to be in front of them.

4. **Get rid of the competitive energy**
There is no doubt that everyone who became a manager had to compete with coworkers to some degree. However, this same aggressive energy isn't helpful when managing a team. When a manager competes against employees or constantly seeks to get all of the glory, they become ineffective and lose all hope of influencing their team. Instead of wanting to always win, look for ways to mentor employees and invest in their growth.

5. **Teach employees to fail forward**
It isn't the manager's job to step in when an employee has made a mistake. Part of teaching employees to be accountable for their actions is to encourage them to fail forward. This entails finding solutions (even if they

are temporary) for problems they are faced with. Not only will this help them learn from their mistakes and reduce the risk of repeating them, but they will also feel a sense of responsibility for their job, which can increase work satisfaction.

6. **Ask employees how they want to be managed**
Seeking feedback from employees is another way to curb micromanagement. Instead of assuming that every person on your team is comfortable with your management style, take the time to sit with each person and ask them how they would like to be managed. For example, some employees who need guidance and reassurance may be comfortable with a weekly check-in, while others who are independent may prefer a bi-weekly or monthly check-in. Yes, adjusting your management style to suit each person requires more work, but it can significantly boost your team's performance.

If there is one thing you can take away from these strategies, it is the need to step back and manage from behind, like a shepherd leading a flock of sheep. You are close enough to respond to crises and offer support but won't get in the way of your employees doing what they are paid to do.

Creating a Culture of Ownership

CB Insights, a data analytics company, helps companies understand the latest industry insights and make informed decisions. Since analysis is a big component of their business, it is important for them to hire employees who take the initiative to learn about upcoming and new technologies in various markets. They place a heavy focus on employee growth and learning by investing in training programs and offering education stipends to those who would like to further their studies. Managers will regularly sit down with employees and discuss their career paths and areas where they might need to improve.

Reonomy is an online search engine for commercial property. Part of growing their business involves uncovering new insights and opportunities for clients nationwide. It is important for them to hire employees that are self-starters and can go above and beyond expectations. To promote this kind of attitude, they frequently announce individual and team "shout outs" during meetings for those who have performed well. They also deliberately recruit people who are passionate about their product, so they can feel connected to the job they are doing (Reiners, 2022).

These two companies are competing in different sectors of the economy, but they have one thing in common—both of them promote a culture of ownership. You may or may not have heard about the "ownership culture." This refers to a work culture where employees are encouraged to take the initiative, solve their own problems, and invest in their personal growth.

Ownership cultures are what drive innovation and high performance in some of the leading companies in the industry. Without employees who are driven to actively participate and take on responsibility, organizations need to constantly spend time and money pushing workers. Of course, support must be available to employees at all times, but in ownership cultures, there is an expectation for employees to reach a stage where they can figuratively take their "training wheels off" and ride their bicycles into the sunset.

One of the first lessons employees will learn when stepping into this type of culture is the difference between internal and external locus of control. Having an internal locus of control means that you are empowered to do what you can with what you have available to you. In contrast, having an external locus of control means that you rely on other people to tell you what you can and cannot do with what you have available to you.

This may also affect your attitude toward work. Someone with an internal locus of control will feel personally responsible for their successes and failures, whereas someone with an external locus of control will see their successes and failures as products of their environment. Out of the two, the person with an internal locus of control is more likely to take initiative in correcting their mistakes than the one who is looking for help or answers externally.

If you read a book about any successful individual, business, or country, you will notice that positive change occurred the moment they started to take responsibility for things within their control and ignored things outside of their control. Inside ownership cultures, you will not find managers who make decisions on behalf of employees or company policies that are so stringent that they prevent employees from applying their own minds to problem-solving. Instead, what you will find are managers who play more of a coaching or supportive role than being supervisors and company values that encourage individuality, free thought, and of course, ownership. Employees will also be expected to be proactive and do whatever they feel needs to be done in order to meet company objectives.

There are a few ways to tell if you have an ownership culture or not. Simply observe how your employees approach their work. Here are a few comparisons to consider:

- Working diligently to meet short deadlines vs. Complaining about the little time they have to complete work.

- Doing the best with the resources they have vs. Waiting on a manager to give instructions or respond to their questions.

- Openness to acquiring more skills and knowledge vs. Being content with the skills and knowledge they already possess.

- Asking the manager for ways to improve performance vs. Continuing to perform poorly without taking the steps to find out what they can do differently.

- Researching how to solve problems in the absence of the manager vs. Pausing work until the manager returns and can solve the problem on their behalf.

- Taking responsibility when the team doesn't perform well vs. Pointing fingers or playing the victim to avoid facing the consequences.

The good news is that you can adopt an ownership culture by teaching your employees how to take action and show commitment toward their career development. Below are a few strategies that can be incorporated into your existing culture:

Promote Information Sharing

The first step to creating a culture of ownership is providing employees with access to information. From the onboarding stage, employees should be given links to resources that explain a wide range of company functions and processes. They should also be given access to company research and reports (depending on their roles) so that they understand the company's strategic aims and how to make a valuable contribution.

Regularly Share the Company's Purpose

Earlier in the book, I shared a story about the janitor working at NASA headquarters who believed that he was part of the mission to send a man to the moon. The benefit of sharing the company's purpose with employees is that they get to associate value with their job and start to believe they are making a positive contribution. This promotes ownership because they are intrinsically motivated to continue to work hard and improve their performance.

Encourage Difference of Opinions

When employees feel comfortable disagreeing with their team members or superiors, they are empowered to think independently and solve their own problems. Create opportunities where teams can sit together and discuss certain topics. Encourage employees to share their opinions, stating why they think that way and what evidence they have to back their claims. Do this on a regular basis to teach them how to think independently and trust their inclinations.

Promote Two-Way Feedback

Two-way feedback encourages employees to review the performance of their managers. When this occurs, managers are able to reflect on the level of support given to employees and where they might possibly improve. It also makes employees feel motivated to continue doing their best work. The trick to effective two-way feedback is to show employees that you are listening by taking their suggestions into consideration. When they see their ideas implemented or concerns treated with urgency, it can significantly boost their morale.

Teach Employees to Think Like the CEO

Empowered employees are driven and ambitious. A great way to make your employees feel empowered is to give them autonomy. Allow them to make decisions concerning their work tasks without getting involved. This communicates that you trust their decision-making abilities, regardless of the outcome. You can also challenge them to think like the CEO. Ask them to approach their work every day as though they were running the company: How would they structure their day? What tasks would take priority? How would they solve problems? Reward employees who demonstrate leadership and encourage others to do the same.

In Summary

The greatest threat to a positive work culture is micromanagement. Employees thrive when they are trusted to perform their duties with a sense of autonomy. When you identify micromanaging in your organization, see it as an opportunity to train managers on how they ought to interact with employees; instead of monitoring work tasks, they should monitor goals and objectives, and instead of assuming all of the responsibility, they should allow employees to take ownership of their work.

Chapter Sixteen

Go Big On Rewards

People work for money but go the extra mile for recognition, praise and rewards. –Dale Carnegie

Your Employees Need More Recognition

In 2020, US software developer Hubspot was dubbed the "Best Place to Work" by Glassdoor. This victory came after the company implemented what they called the Culture Code a year earlier. The culture code promoted values that made up the acronym HEART: humble, empathetic, adaptable, remarkable, and transparent (Dhamdhere, 2022).

The reason for implementing the Culture Code was to encourage their employees to work toward two goals: global inclusion and being a mission-focused organization. However, the executive team knew that unless their initiative involved employee recognition, it wasn't going to succeed.

How many times in your organization have you made elaborate goals without thinking about how you were going to incentivize employees? I have seen many companies spend millions of dollars on upgrading technology and implementing new systems, but not even 1% of that money on showing appreciation to the team of staff that is expected to increase their work performance and work their tails off to meet new demands.

Employees need more recognition, but not for the reasons you might think. The human brain is wired to seek pleasure and avoid pain. This is how the human species has maintained survival for millions of years. This natural instinct is still alive and active in all of us, and can be triggered in various social contexts, such as the workplace.

Seeking pleasure and avoiding pain explains why you procrastinate doing certain tasks but find it easy to do others. Or why you avoid difficult coworkers and gravitate toward the ones you connect with. It can also explain why employee performance can rise or fall depending on how much recognition they are given. When above-average performance is incentivized, employees are inclined to work harder. How come? Their brains expect some type of reward for the increased effort they are putting in. However, when above-average performance is not incentivized, why would an employee go out of their way to increase their workload?

In her commencement speech given at Harvard University, Oprah Winfrey expressed the extent to which human beings desire recognition—even the most powerful people in our society, who we sometimes think don't need to be validated. Below is an excerpt from her speech (Harvard University, 2013):

In every interview, the common denominator that I found was that—we want to be validated and understood. I have done more than 35000 interviews in my career. Once that camera shuts off, everyone turns to me and inevitably, in their way, asks — "Was that okay?"

I heard it from President George Bush. I heard it from President Barack Obama. I have heard it from heroes and homemakers. I have heard it from victims and perpetrators of crimes. And I have heard it from Beyonce in all of her Beyonce-ness. We all want to know one thing: "Was that okay?" "Do you see me?" "Did you hear from me?" "Did I say anything mean to you?"

What we can learn from Oprah Winfrey's insight is that recognition has very little to do with a person's title or position. Whether you are speaking to an entry-level worker or the CEO of the company, both individuals are waiting with bated breath to hear the words: *You are doing a great job, and I appreciate you.*

Benefits of Employee Rewards and Recognition

There is a strange myth that many leaders seem to believe, which is that rewarding employees *too much* causes them to become entitled. First, I don't believe there is such a thing as "too much" recognition, especially when it is earned. And secondly, showing someone appreciation for their hard work doesn't make them entitled; it simply motivates them to continue pushing beyond their limits. Isn't this what every leader desires?

If you are not sold on the importance of employee rewards and recognition, here are a few reasons why you should be:

- **Increased productivity:** Remember the pain and pleasure instinct? Behavior that is associated with rewards, including positive actions or feelings, is more likely to be repeated because it makes you feel good. As such, when above-average performance is rewarded, it can encourage employees to continue working hard.

- **Enhanced positive moods:** If you have spent a lot of time and effort creating a positive work culture, then you take the atmosphere in the workplace very seriously. Rewarding employees increases their job satisfaction, reduces burnout, and boosts positive emotions at work.

- **Retaining high-performing employees:** When the top performers in your company know how much they are appreciated through regular rewards and recognition, they won't think about leaving anytime soon. Plus, when other employees see that hard work pays off, they will feel motivated to develop their skills and grow within your company.

- **Positive company reputation:** Employees who feel valued and supported at work will want to tell the whole world about how awesome your company is. They will share their positive work experiences with friends and family and even recruit or recommend talented people to you.

- **Better customer experience:** When you take care of your employees, they take care of your business. This is their way of showing loyalty and appreciation for what you do for them. Since customers are an important part of your business, valued employees will go above and beyond to treat your customers with the utmost care.

Types of Employee Rewards and Recognition

When thinking about giving rewards and recognition, I encourage you to think beyond monetary benefits. While this is a great incentive, it isn't the only way to show employees how much they are appreciated. In fact, there are a handful of non-monetary types of rewards and recognition that you can incorporate into your work culture. Some of these include:

1. **Private recognition**
   Private recognition involves reaching out to specific employees and praising them for their outstanding work and achievements. What is great about this type of recognition is that it feels more personal and genuine. It also feels good to have your boss send a custom message or leave a handwritten note on your desk because that doesn't happen every day.

2. **Public recognition**
   Public recognition is praise given to specific employees on public platforms where other employees can share in the celebrations. You can give public recognition by giving a shout out to an employee during a meeting, highlighting their achievements in the company newsletter, or pinning a photo of them on the wall of fame, to name a few. The purpose of making recognition public is to motivate other employees to aspire to achieve the same targets or behaviors.

3. **Celebrating special occasions**
   Another way to show appreciation for employees is to celebrate special occasions with them. This might include making a big deal out of birthdays, employee first days, work anniversaries, completion of important projects, and year-end functions. All of these moments can also be used as an opportunity to reinforce your commitment to making employees

feel seen and accepted at work.

4. **Awards**
Offering awards is a fantastic way to keep employees engaged in the long term. Since receiving an award requires meeting certain requirements, they are also given some sort of a standard or overarching goal to continuously aim for. When creating awards, it is important to think about the desired attitudes and behaviors you would like to see at work and strategically introduce awards that motivate employees to develop those qualities.

Some examples of awards you can introduce include:

- **Employee of the Month Award:** recognizes an employee who outperforms others on a specific month.

- **Rising Star Award:** recognizes an employee whose performance has significantly improved over a certain period.

- **The "A-Team" Award:** recognizes a work team that has done exceptional work on a recent project, such as going above and beyond client expectations.

- **The Wolf of Wall Street Award:** recognizes a master salesman or saleswoman who has closed the most deals within a certain period.

- **Employees' Choice Awards:** award given to an employee who has been recognized by their peers as being a hard worker.

- **The "Like a Boss" Award:** recognizes managers who display outstanding leadership qualities or devotion to company values.

Examples of Companies With Great Rewards and Recognition Programs

It is no coincidence that some of the highest-grossing companies in the world have invested a lot of time and money—others even creating entire departments—into implementing employee rewards and recognition programs. What they have come to realize is that how they treat employees affects the company's profits. Happy employees means fewer staff turnover, less money spent on recruitment and training, and increased productivity.

To inspire you to create your own rewards and recognition program, here is a list of a few companies that have done a brilliant job at making their employees happy:

Airbnb

One of the first shifts Airbnb made to improve employee satisfaction was to change the title of their Chief HR Officer to be the Chief Employee Officer. The mission was to make going to work feel like an experience rather than a duty. Some of the benefits the company introduced included annual $2,000 travel stipends, Airbnb healthcare plans, the ability to work from home, and 3–4 weeks of paid time off (Mirmotahari, 2022).

Zappos

Zappos has various reward and recognition initiatives for employees; however, what is unique about this company is its peer-to-peer recognition program. In efforts to promote collaboration and appreciation of team members, Zappos created a few initiatives where employees can nominate each other for rewards. For instance, the "Coworker Bonus Program" allows employees to nominate each other for a $50 bonus each month, and the "Master of WOW Parking" allows employees to nominate each other for premium parking space (Recognize, n.d.).

HP Inc

During the COVID-19 pandemic, HP Inc maintained employee engagement by hosting virtual events, like online dance parties and cooking classes (hosted by world-renowned chefs). The company also rewards employees for good deeds. For instance, employees can earn a Good Card valued at $50 for spending more than 10 hours per quarter doing volunteer work.

Southwest Airlines

Southwest Airlines has made the Forbes list of America's Best Employers six times (Recognize, n.d.). Part of the reason for their success is their rewards program known as SWAG (Southwest Airlines Gratitude). SWAG is a points system that is used to incentivize employee engagement. Points can be exchanged for travel allowances, guest passes, merchandise, gift cards, and tickets to concerts. What's great about this system is that points do not expire, which means that employees can save them up and exchange them for a meaningful reward.

Cisco

Cisco, as a company, has won many awards for being one of the best places to work. To show how much they value employees, the company invests 1% of its payroll in their rewards and recognition program. Some of the benefits the company offers employees include the "Employee Stock Purchase Program," where employees are allowed to invest up to 10% of their salary buying Cisco stocks (at a discounted rate), and tuition reimbursement, where the company pays back employees for money spent on school fees, lab fees, and books when taking courses at accredited institutions (Cisco, n.d.). Other fun rewards offered include a day off on your birthday, receiving a gift or experience on your first and fifth "Ciscoversary," and job swapping, where you can take on somebody else's role for a temporary or permanent basis.

In Summary

Rewarding and recognizing outstanding performance is necessary to motivate desired workplace behaviors. Employees who feel appreciated will go above and beyond expectations to achieve company objectives. There are various ways to create a culture of rewarding and recognizing employees—many of which don't require spending money. Take the time to think about the unique ways that you can reward employees on an ongoing basis and incentivize high performance.

Conclusion

Many things go into influence. You must have a vision, develop your skills and abilities, know your audience, and plan, but at some point, you must take action. Without action, you have no influence. –Josh Steimle

It is difficult for leaders to reach a consensus about what qualities make a good leader. Each one, drawing from their own experiences, will prescribe a list of traits and values about the characteristics of a good leader. The reason why they cannot seem to produce the same exact list is that they understand leadership through their own perceptions.

Perception is everything in the world of business. What you think and feel about something determines your relationship with it. By changing your perceptions, you can experience a completely different business life.

The title of this book is *The Magnetic Mindset*, but you will notice that there wasn't a chapter on mindset. Of course, this was done to prove a point. Since mindset is a psychological phenomenon, you can only change it by adjusting your psychological beliefs, attitudes, and values. This is why instead of focusing on the mind, we looked at various aspects of your career and business that are impacted by how you think.

To have a magnetic mindset means to be able to attract the goals and desires of your heart. But before this can even be possible, you need to believe in your ability to influence and shape your reality. What you see right now isn't all that your career is cut out to be. In fact, the possibilities of who you can become and what you can achieve are endless. Building the kind of business and work relationships that you dream of requires you to be brave enough to break out of your mold.

We have gone through various characteristics of a magnetic mindset that can help you gain influence among employees, customers, investors, and other members of your network. These characteristics included:

Authenticity: Magnetic leaders understand that to be likable, they must be true to themselves. For them, impressing people means showing vulnerability and being relatable.

Empathy: Magnetic leaders are sensitive enough to know that not everybody thinks or feels like them. They seek to understand the perspectives of others by stepping inside another person's shoes and reflecting on their experiences.

Vision: Magnetic leaders are able to see into the future and create a powerful vision that others desire to join and contribute toward. Their vision is sustainable because it is rooted in core values that inform the activities of the business.

Continuous learning: Magnetic leaders devote themselves to ongoing self-development in order to cultivate better leadership qualities. Some of their best teachers can be friends and mentors within their network or the best teacher of all—failure and losses.

Sociability: Magnetic leaders pride themselves in their ability to build and nurture relationships with others. This is a key part of gaining influence and being able to persuade others with words and actions. They take the time to invest in other people because they trust that these relationships will one day pay off.

Magnetic leaders are not born; they are built through endurance, self-awareness, and discipline. If you would like to adopt a magnetic mindset, particularly as it relates to you leading others, then you will need to practice the strategies outlined in this book over and over again. The aim is to make these strategies so common in your interactions with others that they become second nature.

If you have found this book valuable, please leave a review!

References

Amy. (n.d.). *Top 10 quotes about rewards and recognition*. Blog.awardsnetwork.com. https://blog.awardsnetwork.com/top-10-quotes-rewards-recognition

Anderson, B. (2022, June 23). *Mental wellness and empathy in the workplace*. Www.bamboohr.com. https://www.bamboohr.com/blog/mental-wellness-and-empathy-in-the-workplace

Angle, A. (2018, December 12). *4 Ways to represent your authentic self during public speaking*. Training Industry. https://trainingindustry.com/articles/strategy-alignment-and-planning/4-ways-to-represent-your-authentic-self-during-public-speaking/#:~:text=The%20old%20adages%2C%20%E2%80%9CBe%20yourself

Bahn, C. (2021, October 14). *5 Personal branding myths you need to know*. Www.linkedin.com. https://www.linkedin.com/pulse/5-personal-branding-myths-you-need-know-claire-bahn/

Bakshi, P. (2021, October 26). *How to be more likeable, according to science*. Www.refinery29.com. https://www.refinery29.com/en-gb/how-to-be-likeable-psychology

Baxter-Wright, D. (2017, October 9). *8 Employees reveal what it's like to work at IKEA*. Cosmopolitan. https://www.cosmopolitan.com/uk/interiors/a12808032/what-its-like-to-work-at-ikea/

Beheshti, N. (2019, January 16). *10 Timely statistics about the connection between employee engagement and wellness.* Forbes. https://www.forbes.com/sites/nazbeheshti/2019/01/16/10-timely-statistics-about-the-connection-between-employee-engagement-and-wellness/?sh=6cc35d2e22a0

Benson, K. (2017, October 4). *The magic relationship ratio, according to science.* The Gottman Institute; The Gottman Institute. https://www.gottman.com/blog/the-magic-relationship-ratio-according-science/

Big Picture People. (2019, August 7). *7 Strategies for communicating vision for change.* The Big Picture People. https://thebigpicturepeople.co.uk/blog/communicating-vision/

BrandYourself. (2018, June 29). *51 Personal branding quotes: Powerful advice you can't miss.* Brand Yourself Blog. https://brandyourself.com/blog/branding/personal-branding-quotes/

Brescia University. (2017, June 26). *Interesting psychological phenomena: The Pratfall Effect.* Www.brescia.edu. https://www.brescia.edu/2017/06/pratfall-effect/

Brex. (n.d.). *22 Vision statement examples to help you write your own.* Brex. https://www.brex.com/journal/vision-statement-examples

Bringle, L. (2013, July 20). *A funny story about perspective. In Search of the Great Perhaps.* https://searchfortheperhaps.wordpress.com/2013/07/20/a-funny-story-about-perspective/

Catchpole, Z. (2017, January 19). *Ten reasons why people loved Barack Obama.* Sky News. https://news.sky.com/story/ten-reasons-why-people-loved-barack-obama-10726099

Chancellor, D. (2015, May 5). *The importance of values and vision in the practice of leadership.* Www.linkedin.com. https://www.linkedin.com/pulse/importance-values-vision-leadership-derek-chancellor/

Chodyniecka, E., De Smet, A., Dowling, B., & Mugayar-Baldocchi, M. (2022, March 28). *Money can't buy your employees' loyalty*. McKinsey & Company. https://www.mckinsey.com/capabilities/people-and-organizational-performance/our-insights/the-organization-blog/money-cant-buy-your-employees-loyalty

Chute, R. (2021, June 18). *7 Common examples of customer's pain points*. Selling Revolution. https://sellingrevolution.com/blog/7-common-examples-of-customers-pain-points/

Cisco. (n.d.). *Benefits and perks*. Cisco. https://www.cisco.com/c/en/us/about/careers/we-are-cisco/benefits-and-perks.html#~financial

Coca-Cola Company. (2023). *Purpose and Company Vision*. Www.coca-Colacompany.com. https://www.coca-colacompany.com/company/purpose-and-vision#:~:text=Our%20vision%20is%20to%20craft

Copper Staff. (2019, June 10). *Follow-up sales script ideas that help you close the deal*. Copper. https://www.copper.com/resources/follow-up-sales-call-script

Cugelman, B. (2022, April 24). *The 7 principles of social influence for digital psychology*. Medium. https://uxplanet.org/the-7-principles-of-social-influence-for-digital-psychology-4b48c1410f3f

Dhamdhere, P. (2022, March 31). *The importance and benefits of employee rewards and recognition*. Empuls. https://blog.empuls.io/importance-of-employee-rewards-and-recognition/

Dingle, D. T. (2012, August 6). *Oval office interview with President Barack Obama*. Black Enterprise. https://www.blackenterprise.com/president-obama-interview-small-business-unemployment-exclusive/

Eikenberry, K. (2017, February 13). *Finding common ground: Leadership and communication lessons in a fractured world*. The Kevin Eikenberry Group. https://kevineikenberry.com/communication-interpersonal-skills/finding-common-ground-leadership-and-communication-lessons-in-a-fractured-world/

Enfroy, A. (2020, July 16). *3 Steps to easily implement the challenger sales model into your strategy.* Nimble Blog. https://www.nimble.com/blog/using-challenger-sales-model-for-sales/

Fam, J. (n.d.). *Leadership lessons from Undercover Boss.* Https://Coastalchurch.org/. https://coastalchurch.org/leadership-lessons-from-undercover-boss/

Fisher, D. J. (2021, January 19). *Closing once is dead: Why asking for "next steps" is best.* Blog.hubspot.com. https://blog.hubspot.com/sales/closing-once-is-dead

Focusu. (2021, April 9). *100 Insightful quotes on influence.* FocusU. https://focusu.com/blog/100-insightful-quotes-on-influence/#:~:text=Nothing%20has%20a%20greater%20influence

Forbes Coaches Council. (2018, June 4). *Council post: Try these 12 strategies if you need to stop micromanaging.* Forbes. https://www.forbes.com/sites/forbescoachescouncil/2018/06/04/try-these-12-strategies-if-you-need-to-stop-micromanaging/

Forsey, C. (2019, June 25). *18 Quotes about networking that'll help you connect with people.* Hubspot.com. https://blog.hubspot.com/marketing/networking-quotes

Gallo, C. (2018, October 8). *A long-time Apple designer reveals Steve Jobs' 6-step rehearsal process he used for every.* Incafrica.com. https://incafrica.com/library/carmine-gallo-a-long-time-apple-designer-reveals-steve-jobs-6-step-rehearsal-process-he-used-for-every-presentation

Gallup. (2016, April 21). *Presidential approval ratings -- Barack Obama.* Gallup.com. https://news.gallup.com/poll/116479/barack-obama-presidential-job-approval.aspx

Goleman, D. (n.d.). *4 Emotional intelligence skills for handling crises.* Www.kornferry.com. https://www.kornferry.com/insights/this-week-in-leadership/emotional-intelligence-skills-coronavirus-leadership

Good Reads. (n.d.-a). *George R.R. Martin quote.* Www.goodreads.com. https://www.goodreads.com/author/show/346732.George_R_R_Martin

Good Reads. (n.d.-b). *Gina Greenlee quote*. Www.goodreads.com. https://www.goodreads.com/author/show/222416.Gina_Greenlee

Good Reads. (n.d.-c). *Hermann Sudermann quote*. Www.goodreads.com. https://www.goodreads.com/author/show/874992.Hermann_Sudermann

Good Reads. (n.d.-d). *Michelle Tillis Lederman quote*. Www.goodreads.com. https://www.goodreads.com/author/show/5029730.Michelle_Tillis_Lederman

Good Reads. (n.d.-e). *Micromanagement Quotes (16 quotes)*. Www.goodreads.com. https://www.goodreads.com/quotes/tag/micromanagement#:~:text=%E2%80%9CAuthority%E2%80%94when%20abused%20through%20micromanagement

Good Reads. (n.d.-f). *Simon Sinek quote*. Www.goodreads.com. https://www.goodreads.com/author/show/3158574.Simon_Sinek

Good Reads. (n.d.-g). *Stan Slap quote*. Www.goodreads.com. https://www.goodreads.com/author/show/3402756.Stan_Slap

Gregoire, C. (2013, November 18). *What your "life story" really says about you*. HuffPost. https://www.huffpost.com/entry/how-your-life-story-is-a_n_4284006

GrowthForce. (n.d.). *Micromanagement may be destroying your business*. Www.growthforce.com. https://www.growthforce.com/blog/micromanagement-may-be-destroying-your-business#:~:text=When%20you%20micromanage%2C%20you%20actively

Guglielmo, C. (2021, October 23). *What it was like to watch Steve Jobs introduce the iPod 20 years ago*. CNET. https://www.cnet.com/tech/mobile/what-it-was-like-to-watch-steve-jobs-introduce-the-ipod-20-years-ago/

Harvard University. (2013). *Oprah Winfrey Harvard commencement speech*. In YouTube. https://www.youtube.com/watch?v=GMWFieBGR7c

How to find common ground with anyone. (2020, November 11). Worst-Case Scenario. https://www.worstcasescenario.com/blog/how-to-find-common-ground-with-anyone

Huxtable, R. J. (2013, October 1). *Get unstuck: Stop believing the negative stories you tell yourself.* Tiny Buddha. https://tinybuddha.com/blog/get-unstuck-stop-believing-the-negative-stories-you-tell-yourself/

Indeed Editorial Team. (2020, March 31). *What is work culture?* Indeed Career Guide. https://www.indeed.com/career-advice/career-development/work-culture

Indeed Editorial Team. (2021, February 8). *Empathic listening: Definition, examples and tips.* Indeed Career Guide. https://www.indeed.com/career-advice/career-development/empathic-listening

Indeed Editorial Team. (2023a, February 4). *Customer pain points: 4 Examples and how to eliminate them.* Indeed. https://www.indeed.com/career-advice/career-development/customer-pain-points

Indeed Editorial Team. (2023b, March 11). *Cognitive dissonance in marketing: Definition and examples.* Indeed Career Guide. https://www.indeed.com/career-advice/career-development/cognitive-dissonance-marketing#:~:text=What%20is%20cognitive%20dissonance%20in

iSight. (n.d.). *6 Core values exercises for determining your ethics culture.* I-Sight. https://www.i-sight.com/resources/6-core-values-exercises-for-defining-your-companys-ethics-culture/

Kholghi, B. (2020, October 28). *11 Steps to rewrite your story and change your life.* Online Coaching. https://www.coaching-online.org/rewrite-your-story/

Kocienda, K. (2019). *Creative selection : Inside Apple's design process during the golden age of Steve Jobs.* Picador.

Leading Effectively Staff. (2020, March 10). *The best ways to communicate your organization's vision.* CCL. https://www.ccl.org/articles/leading-effectively-articles/communicating-the-vision/#:~:text=A%20vision%20has%20to%20be

Lippert, S. (2020, October 1). *10 Ways to create a culture of ownership at your company.* Www.linkedin.com. https://www.linkedin.com/pulse/10-ways-create-culture-ownership-your-company-scott-lippert

Loew, I. (2020, November 30). *The art of the sales follow-up: 7 Ways to keep the conversation going.* Blog.hubspot.com. https://blog.hubspot.com/sales/sales-follow-up-infographic

Mares, J. (2021, May 13). *A 5-minute summary of "The challenger sale" book your boss told you to read.* Hubspot.com. https://blog.hubspot.com/sales/challenger-sale-summary

Martinez, V. N. (2023, February 14). *Why aligning your leadership style and values is critical for leadership.* Entrepreneur. https://www.entrepreneur.com/leadership/why-aligning-your-leadership-style-and-values-is-critical/443814

Mathur, S. (2020, April 16). *Your approach to meet influential people.* Www.linkedin.com. https://www.linkedin.com/pulse/your-approach-meet-influential-people-salil-mathur/

Maxwell, J. (2016, August 30). *The 5 levels of leadership.* John Maxwell. https://www.johnmaxwell.com/blog/the-5-levels-of-leadership1/

Maxwell, J. C. (2013). *The 5 levels of leadership : Proven steps to maximise your potential.* Center Street.

McCormick, K. (2022, November 24). *How to ask for reviews (with examples!).* Www.wordstream.com. https://www.wordstream.com/blog/ws/2020/07/16/how-to-ask-for-reviews

Mejia, Z. (2017, September 12). *3 Presentation tricks Steve Jobs used that can help you be a better public speaker.* CNBC. https://www.cnbc.com/2017/09/12/3-tricks-steve-jobs-used-that-can-help-you-be-a-better-public-speaker.html

Michail, J. (2020, August 24). *Council post: Strong nonverbal skills matter now more than ever in this "new normal."* Forbes. https://www.forbes.com/sites/forbescoachescouncil/2020/08/24/strong-nonverbal-skills-matter-now-more-than-ever-in-this-new-normal/?sh=72e1d8fc5c61

Mirmotahari, T. (2022, August 11). *7 Awesome Airbnb employee benefits and perks that win employees over.* Www.perkupapp.com. https://www.perkupapp.com/post/7-awesome-airbnb-employee-benefits-perks-that-win-employees-over

Morgan Stanley. (n.d.). *How to create an ownership culture.* Morgan Stanley. https://www.morganstanley.com/atwork/articles/created-ownership-culture

Motherhood Community. (2020, November 6). *How to stop making assumptions in life, relationships, and work.* Motherhood Community. https://motherhoodcommunity.com/how-to-stop-making-assumptions-in-life-relationships-work/

Murphy, M. (2020, June 17). *Cognitive dissonance.* Leadership IQ. https://www.leadershipiq.com/blogs/leadershipiq/cognitive-dissonance

Neale, P. (2019, May 30). *Networking for leaders: 7 Reasons why you need to network!* Unabridged Leadership. https://unabridgedleadership.com/networking-for-leaders-7-reasons-why-you-need-to-network/

O.C. Tanner. (2022). *8 Great types of workplace culture explained.* O.C. Tanner. https://www.octanner.com/culture-glossary/types.html

Peek, S. (2022, August 3). *What is a vision statement?* Business News Daily. https://www.businessnewsdaily.com/3882-vision-statement.html

Recognize. (n.d.). *Companies with the best employee recognition programs.* Recognizeapp.com. https://recognizeapp.com/cms/articles/companies-with-the-best-employee-recognition-programs

Reiners, B. (2022, November 22). *Culture kings: 25 Company culture examples to get you inspired.* Built In. https://builtin.com/company-culture/company-culture-examples

Ricci, T. (2022, October 26). *Public speaking: Know your audience.* Asme.org. https://www.asme.org/topics-resources/content/public-speaking-know-your-audience

Rufferty, I. (2018, January 3). *5 Techniques of social influence that you need to know*. BSG SMS. https://medium.com/bsg-sms/5-techniques-of-social-influence-that-you-need-to-know-9f3fb239495f

S, P. (2018, April 11). *Steve Jobs presents the "1984" ad at the Macintosh pre-launch event (1983) (Transcript)*. The Singju Post. https://singjupost.com/steve-jobs-presents-the-1984-ad-at-the-macintosh-pre-launch-event-1983-transcript/

Sampath, V. (2021, July 25). *Do you need to be approved? Do you have to belong? Do you need that validation?* Www.linkedin.com. https://www.linkedin.com/pulse/do-you-need-approved-have-belong-validation-veena-sampath/

Schwantes, M. (2018, July 2). *6 Uncommon traits of great leaders most people would die to work for*. Incafrica.com. https://incafrica.com/library/marcel-schwantes-6-uncommon-traits-of-great-leaders-most-people-would-die-to-work-for

Schwantes, M. (2019, February 11). *Bill Gates, Steve Jobs, and Warren Buffett all agree: These 3 hiring strategies will land you the best people*. Incafrica.com. https://incafrica.com/library/marcel-schwantes-bill-gates-steve-jobs-agree-these-2-brilliant-hiring-strategies-will-land-you-best-people

SoloFire. (2020, March 25). *60 Motivational sales quotes to fire up your sales reps*. VerbTEAMS. https://solofire.com/blog/60-motivational-sales-quotes-to-fire-up-your-sales-reps/

Spencer, L. (2021, March 23). *What is public speaking? And why is it important?* Business Envato Tuts+. https://business.tutsplus.com/tutorials/what-is-public-speaking--cms-31255

Stobierski, T. (2019, December 4). *How leaders develop and use their network*. Business Insights. https://online.hbs.edu/blog/post/importance-of-networking-in-leadership

Strachan, C. (2020, April 30). *How to build a culture of ownership and accountability*. Grindstone Capital. https://grindstonecapital.co.uk/how-build-culture-ownership-accountability/

Strategic Essentials. (n.d.). *Self-image and effective leadership.* Strategic Essentials. https://strategicessentials.com/motivation/self-image-and-effective-leadership/

Studocu. (2017). *[Transcript] Steve Jobs' 2005 Stanford commencement address.* Studocu.https://www.studocu.com/en-us/document/stanford-university/managerial-economics/transcript-steve-jobs-2005-stanford-commencement-address/32207389

StudyCorgi. (2022, December 24). *Steve Jobs: The Commencement Ceremony speech.* StudyCorgi.com. https://studycorgi.com/steve-jobs-the-commencement-ceremony-speech/

Sudbrink, L. (2022, April 22). *Emotional intelligence is an important part of strong leadership.* Business Leadership Today. https://businessleadershiptoday.com/emotional-intelligence-is-an-important-part-of-strong-leadership/#:~:text=Emotional%20intelligence%20is%20important%20in

Surdek, S. (2016, November 17). *Council post: Why understanding other perspectives is a key leadership skill.* Forbes. https://www.forbes.com/sites/forbescoachescouncil/2016/11/17/why-understanding-other-perspectives-is-a-key-leadership-skill/?sh=7af1b11f6d20

Tappana, J. (2021, November 18). *6 Ways you can use validation to better lead your employees.* Altitude Counseling. https://altitudecounseling.com/validation-communicate-with-employees/

Taubenfeld, E. (2021, November 17). *114 Inspiring leadership quotes to fuel your success.* Reader's Digest. https://www.rd.com/article/leadership-quotes/

Thompson, S. (2021, March 2). *How to analyse your audience before a presentation.* Virtualspeech.com. https://virtualspeech.com/blog/audience-analysis-speech

TrackingTime. (2021, December 6). *10 Types of employee recognition and rewards for your team.* TrackingTime. https://trackingtime.co/best-practices/10-types-of-employee-recognition-and-rewards-for-your-team.html

Tracy, B. (2016, September 22). *30 Motivational sales quotes to inspire success.* Brian Tracy's Self Improvement & Professional Development Blog. https://www.briantracy.com/blog/sales-success/motivational-sales-quotes-for-success/

Tyre, D. (2023, February 9). *How to learn customer pain points.* Blog.hubspot.com. https://blog.hubspot.com/sales/uncover-business-pain#:~:text=Pain%20points%20are%20persistent%20problems

Valle, V. (2021, March). *8 Best examples of personal branding for business leaders.* Latinpresarios. https://latinpresarios.com/best-examples-of-personal-branding/

Vantage Circle. (2019, March 15). *30 Thought-provoking company culture quotes.* Vantage Circle HR Blog. https://blog.vantagecircle.com/company-culture-quotes/

Vormschlag, J. (n.d.). *How to determine a company's culture in three easy steps.* Www.veristat.com. https://www.veristat.com/blog/how-to-determine-a-companys-culture-in-three-easy-steps

Wenderoth, M. C. (2019, December 16). *How to network with powerful people.* Harvard Business Review. https://hbr.org/2019/12/how-to-network-with-powerful-people

Wiener, J. (2021, February 8). *Sell me this pen. I tackle the Wolf of Wall Street sales riddle. Do you know the right way to sell the pen?* The Kickass Entrepreneur. https://www.thekickassentrepreneur.com/sell-me-this-pen-i-tackle-the-wolf-of-wall-street-sales-riddle-do-you-know-the-right-way-to-sell-the-pen/

Williams, B. (2020). *21 Mind-blowing sales stats.* Thebrevetgroup.com. https://blog.thebrevetgroup.com/21-mind-blowing-sales-stats

Winter, C. (2022, November 25). *How to stop making assumptions: 8 Highly effective tips.* A Conscious Rethink. https://www.aconsciousrethink.com/20390/how-to-stop-making-assumptions/

Also By
Thomas Allan

You can subscribe to my weekly blog, where I cover topics relating to magnetic mindset, leadership, influence, persuasion and much more. I also offer from time-to-time free workbooks and ebooks.

https://magneticmindsetblog.com/

About Author

Thomas Allan

Introducing Thomas Allan, the visionary author of "The Magnetic Mindset: Unlocking the Secrets of Influence & Persuasion." Thomas has spent over 30 years consulting with high-performing organizations and individuals as a growth mindset advocate and leadership development expert. Known for his electrifying speaking and training engagements, Thomas brings his knowledge of the magnetic mindset, leadership, and personal growth to audiences worldwide.

In "The Magnetic Mindset," Thomas combines his deep understanding of growth mindset principles with expertise in leadership development to provide readers with a transformative guide to becoming effective and influential leaders. By exploring the secrets of influence and persuasion, this comprehensive resource offers practical strategies and insights that empower anyone to adopt a growth mindset and become a magnetic leader.

Drawing from diverse real-world examples, Thomas demystifies the art of leadership, breaking it down into accessible, actionable steps. Focusing on crucial growth mindset concepts such as embracing challenges, cultivating resilience, and fostering continuous learning, "The Magnetic Mindset" equips readers with the tools they need to lead with confidence and authority. By integrating cutting-edge research on brain plasticity and the power of self-belief, Thomas shows how anyone can develop the mindset and skills required for effective leadership.

Whether you're an aspiring leader seeking to unlock your potential or an experienced manager looking to elevate your leadership skills, "The Magnetic Mindset" is the ultimate guide to mastering the art of influence and persuasion. Immerse yourself in this transformative book and discover how the magnetic mindset can help you excel personally and professionally.

Thomas also writes a weekly blog article and provides free resources to help individuals develop mindset skills. Subscribe at:

https://magneticmindsetblog.com/

www.ingramcontent.com/pod-product-compliance
Lightning Source LLC
Chambersburg PA
CBHW070257010526
44107CB00056B/2489